200 *Fast*
chicken dishes

hamlyn | **all colour cookbook**

200 *Fast*
chicken dishes

An Hachette UK Company

www.hachette.co.uk

First published in Great Britain in 2015 by Hamlyn
a division of Octopus Publishing Group Ltd, Carmelite
House, 50 Victoria Embankment, London, EC4Y 0DZ

www.octopusbooks.co.uk

Copyright © Octopus Publishing Group Ltd 2015

Some of the recipes in this book have previously appeared
in other titles published by Hamlyn.

ISBN : 978-0-600-62900-9

A CIP catalogue record for this book is available
from the British Library.

Printed and bound in China

10 9 8 7 6 5 4 3 2

Both metric and imperial measurements have been given
in all recipes. Use one set of measurements only, and not a
mixture of both.

Standard level spoon measurements are used in all recipes.
1 tablespoon = 15 ml spoon
1 teaspoon = 5 ml spoon

Ovens should be preheated to the specified temperature
– if using a fan-assisted oven, follow the manufacturer's
instructions for adjusting the time and temperature.

Fresh herbs should be used unless otherwise stated.

Eggs should be medium unless otherwise stated. The
Department of Health advises that eggs should not be
consumed raw. This book contains dishes made with raw
or lightly cooked eggs. It is prudent for more vulnerable
people such as pregnant and nursing mothers, invalids, the
elderly, babies and young children to avoid uncooked or
lightly cooked dishes made with eggs. Once prepared these
dishes should be kept refrigerated and used promptly.

This book includes dishes made with nuts and nut
derivatives. It is advisable for customers with known
allergic reactions to nuts and nut derivatives and those who
may be potentially vulnerable to these allergies, such as
pregnant and nursing mothers, invalids, the elderly, babies
and children, to avoid dishes made with nuts and nut
oils. It is also prudent to check the labels of pre-prepared
ingredients for the possible inclusion of nut derivatives.

contents

introduction

This book offers a new and flexible approach to meal-planning for busy cooks and lets you choose the recipe option that best fits the time you have available. Inside you will find 200 dishes that will inspire you and motivate you to get cooking every day of the year.

All the recipes take a maximum of 30 minutes to cook. Some take as little as 20 minutes and, amazingly, many take only 10 minutes.

On every page you'll find a main recipe plus a short-cut version or a fancier variation if you have a bit more time to spare. Whatever you go for, you'll find a huge range of super-quick recipes to get you through the week.

chicken dishes

Chicken is inexpensive, quick to cook and hugely versatile, and its mild flavour makes it a favourite with people of every age. The unending appeal of chicken as a source of protein lies in its mild flavour, which lends itself to being blended with a host of different ingredients, from the delicate tastes of Mediterranean foods, such as basil and olives, to the rich, heavily spiced stews and curries of India. This is why we find chicken in so many recipes from around the globe, and why we have been able to include so many exciting and different recipes in this book. Think of chicken as a blank canvas to which you can add your favourite flavours. Chicken works with almost every style of cooking: Asian-style stir-fries; garlicky or herby grilled dishes; richly spiced curries; warm and cold salads; fragrant Thai coconut recipes; classic coq au vin and other wine-based stews; simple pasta dishes – the opportunities for your evening meal are almost endless.

tips and techniques

There a few simple cooking aids that really can have an amazing effect on the time spent in the kitchen.

• A food processor and a mini chopper are great time-savers.

- A good vegetable peeler, garlic peeler and crusher are all great, simple little gadgets to help save time on fiddly jobs.

- Good, sharp knives make food preparation simpler and faster.

- Try cooking large amounts and then freezing in portions. This way, you'll always have a fast, ready-made, low-effort meal at your fingertips.

- Preparing ingredients in advance will save time when you come to cook the meal later on. Peel and chop vegetables, for example, then keep them refrigerated in freezer bags until you need them.

a speedy food

Chicken appeals to cooks for many reasons, not least because it freezes exceptionally well (a chicken can be frozen with no effect on its flavour or texture for up to two years). But its unending value as an ingredient in so many dishes can be found in the speed with which it can be cooked.

A whole bird, no matter how small, cannot be cooked in less than an hour of course, but you should be able to cook the individual parts of the chicken – a wing, a leg, a thigh or a breast – within 30 minutes. When you are buying thighs, it can be worth paying a little bit more to get them already deboned, so that you can flatten the meat or cut the flesh into chunks and thereby speed up the cooking process. If the recipe requires that you keep

the thighs whole, try to buy smaller thighs, because the larger they are, the longer they will take to cook. If small or boneless thighs are unavailable, you can speed up the cooking process by making a few fairly deep cuts into the surface of the meat. The same is true with chicken breast: flatten or score the meat and it will cook much quicker.

When preparing recipes that call for small pieces of chicken breast, many people choose to use mini-fillets. These tend to be extremely tender and incredibly easy to cook, so they may be worth the extra money.

With the growth in demand for ready-prepared foods, you can now find chicken in a host of

low in fat, as long as you are careful about the amount of oil you put in the pan. The key to a successful low-fat diet is to mix up the flavours in your meals so that you never get bored: expand your repertoire and try out some new recipes.

Although chicken wings technically qualify as white meat as well, you should be aware that they are also the fattiest part of the bird. Be careful when you are barbecuing wings: they are prone to flare up because of the amount of fat that comes out when they cook. Chicken thighs and legs are still lean meat compared to meats such as beef and lamb, however. If you are watching your calorific intake, always make sure to remove the chicken skin, as the majority of the fat is stored just under the skin.

different flavours. If you look in a delicatessen or the cooked meat aisle of a supermarket, you can find smoked chicken breast, which is wonderful in salads and on pizzas, Tikka-flavoured cooked chicken pieces, which are excellent in sandwiches, and other interesting flavours, including Chinese chicken, barbecue-flavoured chicken and Cajun chicken.

a healthy choice

Another reason why chicken breast is such a popular choice these days is that it contains little fat. Steamed or grilled chicken breast is one of the leanest, healthiest meats available, and even stir-fried chicken can be

great for family and friends

It seems that everybody likes chicken. When you are entertaining a large number of guests, you can almost guarantee that a chicken dish will be particularly well received. Similarly, when you are cooking for a roomful of youngsters, be they three or thirteen years old, chicken recipes will usually go down well with even the fussiest of young diners. So defrost those chicken pieces you've got in the freezer, choose one of our gorgeous recipes and dish up a delicious feast for your family and friends in next to no time at all. No matter which recipe you choose from this book today, it is bound to be a sure-fire winner.

snacks &
light bites

creamy herby chicken on bagels

Serves **4**
Total cooking time **30 minutes**

4 **bagels**, halved
25 g (1 oz) **ready-made garlic
    butter**, softened
2 tablespoons **olive oil**
1 small **onion**, chopped
2 **skinless chicken breast
    fillets**, sliced
175 g (6 oz) **chestnut
    mushrooms**, quartered
2 tablespoons **sherry**
200 ml (7 fl oz) **crème fraîche**
2 tablespoons chopped
    parsley
salt and **pepper**

Place the bagel halves, cut side up, on a baking sheet, spread over the garlic butter and bake in a preheated oven, 190°C (375°F), Gas Mark 5, for 10–15 minutes until crisp.

Meanwhile, heat the oil in a frying pan, add the onion and cook for 3 minutes. Add the chicken and cook for 5 minutes. Add the mushrooms cook for a further 5 minutes until tender. Add the sherry and allow to bubble, then stir in the crème fraîche and parsley and season with salt and pepper. Simmer, stirring, adding a little water if the mixture is too thick, until the chicken is cooked through. Spoon over the baked bagels and serve.

For garlic baked mushrooms with chicken, put 4 large portobello mushrooms, stalk sides up, on a baking sheet. Dot with 25 g (1 oz) ready-made garlic butter, season with salt and pepper and bake in a preheated oven, 200°C (400°F), Gas Mark 6, for 15 minutes until tender. Meanwhile, fry 1 small onion and 2 chopped skinless chicken breast fillets in 1 tablespoon olive oil for 5 minutes. Stir in 200 ml (7 fl oz) crème fraîche and 2 tablespoons chopped parsley. Season with salt and pepper and simmer for 5 minutes, adding a little water if the mixture becomes too thick, until the chicken is cooked through. Spoon over the baked garlicky mushrooms to serve. **Total cooking time 20 minutes.**

cajun chicken & avocado melt

Serves **2**
Total cooking time **10 minutes**

1 small **ciabatta loaf**, halved
    lengthways
2 tablespoons **tomato
    chutney**
2 **tomatoes**, sliced
100 g (3½ oz) **ready-cooked
    Cajun-spiced chicken
    breast**, sliced
1 small **avocado**, stoned,
    peeled and sliced
150 g (5 oz) **mozzarella
    cheese**, sliced

Put the ciabatta halves, cut side down, on a foil-lined grill pan and toast under a preheated medium grill for a few minutes until crisp and hot. Turn over the bread and spread with the tomato chutney. Arrange the tomato slices on top, followed by the chicken, avocado and finally the mozzarella.

Place under the grill and cook for 5 minutes or until the cheese has melted and the topping is hot.

For Cajun chicken 'rarebit', mix together 200 g (7 oz) grated mature Cheddar cheese, 1 teaspoon Cajun seasoning mix, a pinch of cayenne pepper, ½ beaten egg and 1 tablespoon beer. Toast 2 large slices of crusty bread on both sides, top with 1 sliced ready-cooked chicken breast and 2 sliced tomatoes. Spread the cheese mixture over the top and cook under the grill until golden and bubbling. **Total cooking time 10 minutes.**

chicken & goats' cheese panini

Serves **4**
Total cooking time **20 minutes**

4 tablespoons **ready-made pesto**
1 tablespoon **olive oil**
4 **panini rolls** or **4 part-baked baguettes**, halved
2 **ready-cooked chicken breasts**, sliced
125 g (4 oz) **sun-dried tomatoes in oil**, drained
200 g (7 oz) **goats' cheese**, sliced
handful of **basil leaves**

Mix together the pesto and oil and brush over the cut side of the bottom halves of the panini rolls or baguettes. Top with the sliced chicken, sun-dried tomatoes, goats' cheese and basil. Cover with the top half of the rolls or baguettes.

Cook in a sandwich toaster or panini grill for about 5 minutes until the bread is crisp and the filling is hot. Alternatively, cook in a hot pan or griddle, pressing the rolls down firmly. Turn and cook on the other side.

For chicken & goats' cheese pizza, spread 4 tablespoons tomato pizza topping sauce over a large ready-made pizza base. Top with 2 sliced ready-cooked chicken breasts, 125 g (4 oz) sliced goats' cheese and a handful of black olives. Drizzle over 1 tablespoon pesto mixed with 1 tablespoon olive oil and bake in a preheated oven, 200°C (400°F), Gas Mark 6, for 15 minutes or until the base is crisp and the topping is hot. **Total cooking time 20 minutes.**

chicken quesadillas

Serves **4**

Total cooking time **30 minutes**

8 **soft flour tortillas**

220 g (7½ oz) can **refried beans**

250 g (8 oz) **ready-cooked chicken**, chopped

1 **red chilli**, deseeded and finely chopped

4 **tomatoes**, finely chopped

handful of **fresh coriander**, roughly chopped

175 g (6 oz) **mature Cheddar cheese**, grated

3 tablespoons **olive oil**

lettuce and sweetcorn salad, to serve

Spread 4 of the tortillas with the refried beans, top with the cooked chicken, chopped chilli, tomatoes, coriander and grated cheese. Cover with the remaining tortillas, pressing them together firmly.

Heat 1 tablespoon of the olive oil in a large frying pan, add 1 quesadilla and fry for 3 minutes on each side until the cheese has melted and the quesadilla is golden and crisp. Remove from the pan and keep warm. Repeat with the remaining quesadillas, adding a little more oil as necessary.

Cut into wedges and serve warm with crisp lettuce and sweetcorn salad.

For chilli chicken nachos, spread 150 g (5 oz) tortilla chips in the bottom of a large ovenproof dish. Dot with 220 g (7½ oz) can refried beans, 175 g (6 oz) chopped ready-cooked chicken and 4 tablespoons spicy tomato salsa. Sprinkle over 125 g (4 oz) grated Cheddar cheese and place under a preheated medium grill until the cheese has melted. Sprinkle with chopped fresh coriander and serve. **Total cooking time 10 minutes.**

chicken salsa wraps

Serves **4**

Total cooking time **10 minutes**

200 g (7 oz) **fresh tomato salsa**

4 **soft flour tortillas**

250 g (8 oz) **ready-cooked barbecue-flavoured chicken**, chopped

¼ small **red cabbage**, shredded

2 **carrots**, coarsely grated

4 **spring onions**, cut into fine strips

150 ml (¼ pint) **soured cream**

green salad, to serve

Spoon the tomato salsa on to the tortillas and spread it evenly. Place a quarter of the chicken in the centre of each one with some of the cabbage, carrots and spring onions.

Top with soured cream and roll up. Cut in half and serve with a green salad.

For balsamic chicken wraps, thinly slice 3 skinless chicken breast fillets and coat in a mixture of 2 tablespoons balsamic vinegar, 2 tablespoons olive oil and 1 crushed garlic clove. Season with salt and pepper. Cook the chicken, in batches, on a hot griddle or in a frying pan for 1–2 minutes on each side until cooked through. Place on warmed soft flour tortillas with 200 g (7 oz) tomato salsa, ¼ small shredded red cabbage, 2 grated carrots and 4 spring onions, cut into strips. Top with soured cream, roll up and serve. **Total cooking time 30 minutes.**

spiced chicken naans

Serves **2**

Total cooking time **30 minutes**

4 tablespoons **natural yogurt**

1 tablespoon **jalfrezi curry paste**

2 tablespoons **lemon juice**

2 **skinless chicken breast fillets**, each cut into 8 pieces

1 small **red onion**, thinly sliced

1 small **green pepper**, cored, deseeded and thinly sliced

4 tablespoons **passata**

2 **garlic and coriander naan breads**

150 g (5 oz) **mozzarella cheese**, sliced

Mix together the yogurt, jalfrezi paste and lemon juice. Add the chicken pieces and stir to coat. Place the chicken on a foil-lined grill pan with the onion and pepper slices and cook under a preheated hot grill for 5–8 minutes, turning occasionally, until the chicken is cooked and beginning to char at the edges and the onion and pepper slices have softened slightly.

Spread the passata over the naan breads, top with the chicken, onion, green pepper and mozzarella. Line the grill pan with a clean piece of foil. Place the naan breads on the foil, reduce the grill to a medium heat and cook the naan 'pizzas' for 5–8 minutes or until the cheese has melted and the topping is hot.

For hot spiced chicken & mango chutney chapati wraps, mix 2 chopped skinless chicken breast fillets with 4 tablespoons natural yogurt, 1 tablespoon jalfrezi paste and 2 tablespoons lemon juice. Transfer to a foil-lined grill pan and cook under a preheated hot grill for 5–8 minutes, turning occasionally, until cooked and beginning to char at the edges. Place on 2 warmed chapatis with 1 thinly sliced small red onion, fresh coriander leaves and 2 tablespoons mango chutney. Roll up the chapatis and serve warm. **Total cooking time 20 minutes.**

chicken BLT

Serves **4**

Total cooking time **10 minutes**

4 **back bacon rashers**

8 **wholemeal bread slices**

2 teaspoons **wholegrain mustard**

4 crisp **iceberg lettuce leaves**

4 **tomatoes**, sliced

2 **ready-cooked chicken breasts**, sliced

1 **avocado**, stoned, peeled and sliced

Fry the bacon rashers in a dry frying pan until crisp.

Meanwhile, toast the wholemeal bread on both sides, then spread 4 slices with the wholegrain mustard.

Place a lettuce leaf on each of these slices and top with the sliced tomato. Divide the chicken between the slices of toast.

Top with the bacon and the avocado.

Finish with the remaining slices of toast and, using cocktail sticks to keep the sandwiches together, cut on the diagonal to serve.

For stuffed chicken breasts, make a slit down the sides of 4 boneless, skinless chicken breasts, about 150 g (5 oz) each, to form pockets. Stuff each pocket with 175 g (6 oz) sliced Fontina cheese and a handful of basil leaves. Wrap each chicken breast with 2 slices of Parma ham. Place on a baking sheet and cook in a preheated oven, 200°C (400°F), Gas Mark 6, for 20 minutes or until cooked through. Meanwhile, heat 2 tablespoons olive oil in a frying pan and toss in 250 g (8 oz) baby spinach leaves and 200 g (7 oz) cherry tomatoes. Cook briefly until the spinach starts to wilt. Serve the chicken breasts on a bed of wilted spinach. **Total cooking time 30 minutes.**

chicken salad wraps

Serves **4**

Total cooking time **10 minutes**

4 **soft flour tortillas**

4 tablespoons **mayonnaise**

4 teaspoons **mango chutney**

2 **carrots**, grated

2 **ready-cooked chicken
breasts**, shredded

¼ small **white cabbage**, thinly
shredded

2 **tomatoes**, sliced

small handful of **fresh
coriander leaves**

salt and **pepper**

Lay the tortillas on the work surface and spread
each one with 1 tablespoon of the mayonnaise and
1 tablespoon of the mango chutney.

Divide the remaining ingredients between the tortillas
and season with salt and pepper. Roll up the wraps to
serve.

For chicken club sandwich, grill 8 unsmoked
streaky bacon rashers under a preheated hot grill for
3–4 minutes on each side until crisp. Toast 12 slices of
bread for 2–3 minutes on each side. Spread 4 slices
of the toast with 2 tablespoons mayonnaise. Top the
slices with some shredded iceberg lettuce, 3 sliced
tomatoes and the bacon. Spread 4 more slices of toast
with 2 tablespoons mango chutney and place on top
of the bacon. Cover the mango with 2 sliced cooked
chicken breasts and 1 thinly sliced small red onion.
Top with the remaining slices of toast and secure each
sandwich with 2 cocktail sticks. Slice in half diagonally
to serve. **Total cooking time 20 minutes.**

mulligatawny in a mug

Serves **4–6**
Total cooking time **10 minutes**

2 tablespoons **vegetable oil**
1 **onion**, coarsely grated
1 **garlic clove**, crushed
3 tablespoons **medium-hot curry paste**
½ teaspoon **ground turmeric**
1 litre (1¾ pints) hot **chicken stock**
1 small **apple**, peeled and grated
500 g (1 lb) **ready-cooked basmati rice**
350 g (11½ oz) **ready-cooked chicken**, torn into bite-sized pieces
100 g (3½ oz) small **croutons**
chopped **fresh coriander**, to garnish

Heat the oil in a large saucepan, add the onion and garlic and cook over a medium-high heat for 3–4 minutes, stirring frequently, until softened.

Add the curry paste and turmeric, stir for 1 minute, then add the stock, apple and rice. Simmer for 3–4 minutes to thicken slightly.

Stir in the chicken, then ladle the mulligatawny into wide mugs. Top with the croutons and the coriander.

For quick chicken mulligatawny, heat 2 tablespoons vegetable oil in a large saucepan and add 1 chopped onion, 2 chopped garlic cloves, 1 chopped carrot and 2 chopped potatoes. Cook over a medium heat for 6–7 minutes, stirring frequently. Stir in 2 tablespoons Madras-style curry paste and cook for 1 minute. Add 1.2 litres (2 pints) hot chicken stock and 1 small, peeled and grated apple. Bring to the boil and simmer for 8–10 minutes until tender. Blend to the desired consistency, or leave chunky, then stir in 250 g (8 oz) ready-cooked basmati rice and 250 g (8 oz) shredded ready-cooked chicken. Ladle into bowls and serve garnished with croutons and fresh coriander, if liked. **Total cooking time 20 minutes.**

ginger chicken soup

Serves **4**
Total cooking time **20 minutes**

1 tablespoon **groundnut oil**
2.5 cm (1 inch) piece of **fresh root ginger**, peeled and grated
300 g (10 oz) **skinless chicken breast fillets**, cut into strips
1 litre (1¾ pints) hot **chicken stock**
4 **pak choi**, sliced
175 g (6 oz) **dried egg noodles**
2 tablespoons **sesame seeds**

Heat the oil in a wok or large saucepan, add the ginger and stir-fry for 1 minute, then stir in the chicken and 125 ml (4 fl oz) of the stock. Bring to the boil, then cook over a high heat for 5 minutes or until the chicken is cooked through.

Add the remaining stock and bring to a simmer. Stir in the pak choi and noodles and simmer for 5 minutes until the noodles are cooked.

Meanwhile, heat a nonstick frying pan over a medium-low heat and dry-fry the sesame seeds for 2 minutes, stirring frequently, until golden brown and toasted.

Ladle the soup into bowls and serve sprinkled with the toasted sesame seeds.

For ginger chicken wraps, heat 1 tablespoon olive oil in a frying pan, add 450 g (14½ oz) thinly sliced skinless chicken breast fillets, 1 tablespoon peeled and grated fresh root ginger, 2 diced garlic cloves and 6 sliced spring onions and fry, stirring, for 5–6 minutes or until the chicken is cooked through. Divide the chicken between 4 tortilla wraps, then top with 1 red and 1 yellow pepper, both cored, deseeded and sliced, and ½ shredded cos (romaine) lettuce. Roll up the wraps and serve. **Total cooking time 10 minutes.**

chicken caesar salad

Serves **4**

Total cooking time **10 minutes**

½ **ciabatta loaf**, cubed

2 tablespoons **olive oil**

1 **cos** (**romaine**) **lettuce**,
   leaves separated

200 g (7 oz) **ready-cooked
   chicken**, chopped

75 g (3 oz) **ready-cooked
   crispy bacon rashers**,
   broken into pieces

6 tablespoons **ready-made
   Caesar salad dressing**

25 g (1 oz) **Parmesan cheese
   shavings**

Place the ciabatta cubes on a foil-lined grill pan and drizzle over the olive oil. Toast under a preheated medium grill for about 5 minutes, turning occasionally, until golden and crisp.

Meanwhile, roughly tear the lettuce leaves and place in a salad bowl with the chicken and most of the bacon pieces.

Add the toasted bread cubes and salad dressing and toss well to mix. Sprinkle over the reserved bacon pieces and the Parmesan shavings. Serve immediately.

For chicken Caesar with garlicky croutons, cut ½ ciabatta loaf into cubes. Mix 1 crushed garlic clove and 4 tablespoons olive oil and toss the cubes in the oil. Spread on a baking sheet and bake in a preheated oven, 200°C (400°F), Gas Mark 6, for 10 minutes until crisp. Add to a bowl of torn cos (romaine) lettuce leaves, chopped ready-cooked chicken and crispy bacon pieces tossed in 6 tablespoons ready-made Caesar salad dressing. **Total cooking time 20 minutes.**

hot & sour chicken salad

Serves **4**
Total cooking time **10 minutes**

250 g (8 oz) **ready-cooked chicken**, roughly chopped
150 g (5 oz) **salad leaves**
125 g (4 oz) **button mushrooms**, thinly sliced
1 **red chilli**, deseeded and finely chopped
1 small bunch of **fresh coriander**, leaves stripped and chopped
1 tablespoon **tom yum paste** or **Thai red curry paste**
4 tablespoons **vegetable oil**
2 tablespoons **lime juice**
2 tablespoons roughly chopped **roasted salted cashew nuts** (optional)

Toss the chicken in a large bowl with the salad leaves, mushrooms, chopped chilli and coriander, then divide between 4 plates.

Place the tom yum paste, vegetable oil and lime juice in a jar with a tight-fitting lid, then shake until thoroughly combined. Drizzle over the salad, scatter over the cashew nuts, if using, and serve immediately.

For hot & sour chicken soup, put 450 ml (¾ pint) chicken stock or water in a large saucepan with 6 tablespoons tom yum paste and bring to the boil. Add 250 g (8 oz) sliced skinless chicken breast fillets, then reduce the heat and simmer for 7–8 minutes until the chicken is cooked through. Stir in 200 ml (7 fl oz) coconut milk and 125 g (4 oz) thinly sliced button mushrooms and simmer for a further 1–2 minutes until the mushrooms are just tender. Ladle into deep bowls, then squeeze over some lime juice and serve garnished with chopped coriander leaves and a finely chopped deseeded red chilli, if liked. **Total cooking time 20 minutes.**

tandoori chicken wings with raita

Serves **4**
Total cooking time **30 minutes**

2 tablespoons **tandoori paste**
1 teaspoon **cumin seeds**
75 ml (3 fl oz) **natural yogurt**
2 teaspoons **lemon juice**
8–12 **chicken wings**, about
    750 g (1½ lb) total weight

Raita
150 g (5 oz) **cucumber**
200 ml (7 fl oz) **natural yogurt**
2 teaspoons **lemon juice**
½ teaspoon **ground cumin**
salt and **pepper**

To serve
½ **iceberg lettuce**, shredded
4–8 **poppadums**

Mix the tandoori paste, cumin seeds, yogurt and lemon juice in a large, shallow dish. Make 2–3 shallow cuts in each chicken wing and place in the dish. Use your fingers to coat the chicken wings thoroughly with the tandoori yogurt.

Arrange the wings in a single layer on a foil-lined baking sheet and cook in a preheated oven, 220°C (425°F), Gas Mark 7, for 20–25 minutes until slightly charred and the juices run clear when the thickest part of the chicken is pierced with a fork.

Meanwhile, make the raita. Halve the piece of cucumber lengthways and use a spoon to remove the seeds. Coarsely grate the flesh and place in the middle of a clean tea towel, then bring up the edges and twist the cucumber in the tea towel over a sink to squeeze out the excess moisture. Place the cucumber in a bowl, add the yogurt, lemon juice and ground cumin, then season to taste and chill until the chicken is cooked.

Serve the cooked chicken wings with the shredded lettuce, chilled raita and crisp poppadums.

For tandoori chicken pittas, mix 1 tablespoon tandoori paste in a bowl with 150 ml (¼ pint) natural yogurt, 1 tablespoon chopped mint, ½ teaspoon ground cumin, 2 teaspoons lemon juice and plenty of salt and pepper. Fold in 300 g (10 oz) diced ready-cooked chicken and stir thoroughly to coat, then spoon into 4 large, warmed wholemeal pitta breads. Add some shredded lettuce and serve immediately. **Total cooking time 10 minutes.**

chicken & courgette kebabs

Serves **4**

Total cooking time **20 minutes**

16 **unsmoked streaky bacon rashers**

2 **courgettes**, each cut into 16 pieces

3 **skinless chicken breast fillets**, each cut into 8 pieces

1 tablespoon **sunflower oil**

2 tablespoons **clear honey**

1 tablespoon **wholegrain mustard**

To serve
sweetcorn
peas

Soak 8 small wooden skewers in water. Stretch each bacon rasher with the back of a knife. Cut each rasher in half and wrap around a piece of courgette. Thread on to 8 skewers, alternating the courgettes with pieces of chicken.

Place the kebabs on a foil-lined grill pan. Warm the oil, honey and mustard together in a small pan, brush over the kebabs and cook under a preheated medium grill for 10 minutes, turning occasionally and brushing with any remaining honey mixture, until the bacon is crisp and the chicken is cooked through. Serve with sweetcorn and peas.

For chicken, bacon & courgette baguettes, cut 2 courgettes into slices lengthways and place on a foil-lined grill pan. Brush the courgettes with a little oil, honey and mustard and grill together with 4 bacon rashers for about 5 minutes until the courgettes are tender and the bacon is crisp. Cut a baguette into 4 pieces and cut in half lengthways. Butter and fill with 250 g (8 oz) sliced ready-cooked chicken and the courgettes and bacon. **Total cooking time 10 minutes.**

lemon, mint & chicken skewers

Serves **4**

Total cooking time **20 minutes**

150 g (5 oz) **Greek yogurt**
finely grated rind and juice of
   1 **lemon**
2 tablespoons chopped **mint**
2 tablespoons **olive oil**
4 **skinless chicken breast**
   fillets, each cut into 8 pieces
salt and **pepper**

To serve
warmed **pitta breads**,
sliced **cucumber**
sliced **radish**

Soak 8 small wooden skewers in water. Mix together the yogurt, lemon rind and juice, mint and olive oil. Add the chicken pieces and stir well to coat.

Thread the chicken on to the skewers and place on a foil-lined grill pan. Cook under a preheated hot grill for about 10 minutes, turning occasionally, or until the chicken is cooked and slightly charred at the edges. Slide the chicken off the skewers and serve in warm pitta breads with slices of cucumber and radish.

For lemon chicken pittas, make a lemon mint dressing by mixing together 2 tablespoons mayonnaise, 2 tablespoons Greek yogurt, 1 teaspoon finely grated lemon rind and 1 tablespoon chopped mint. Warm 4 pitta breads and fill with sliced ready-cooked chicken, sliced cucumber and sliced radish. Top with the lemon mint dressing. **Total cooking time 10 minutes.**

fennel, chicken & tomato pizza

Serves **2**
Total cooking time **30 minutes**

2 tablespoons **olive oil**
1 small **onion**, sliced
1 **garlic clove**, crushed
1 small head of **fennel**, thinly
   sliced
3 **tomatoes**, chopped
pinch of **sugar**
1 tablespoon **tomato purée**
145 g (4½ oz) **pizza base mix**
125 g (4 oz) **ready-cooked**
   chicken, chopped
8 **cherry tomatoes**, halved
150 g (5 oz) **mozzarella**
   cheese, sliced
salt and **pepper**

Heat the olive oil in a frying pan, add the onion, garlic and fennel and cook for 3 minutes. Add the tomatoes, sugar and tomato purée and simmer for 5 minutes until the mixture is soft and pulpy. Season with salt and pepper.

Meanwhile, make the pizza base according to the packet instructions. Knead lightly until smooth, shape into a ball and roll out thinly to a circle about 30 cm (12 inches) across. Place on a baking sheet.

Spread the tomato and fennel sauce over the pizza base and scatter over the chicken and cherry tomatoes. Arrange the mozzarella on top and bake in a preheated oven, 220°C (425°F), Gas Mark 7, for 15 minutes until crisp and golden.

For fennel, chicken & tomato pasta, heat 2 tablespoons olive oil in a pan, add 1 chopped onion, 1 crushed garlic clove, 250 g (8 oz) chopped ready-cooked chicken and 1 chopped small head of fennel. Cook for 3 minutes, then add 3 chopped tomatoes and 150 ml (¼ pint) passata and simmer for 5 minutes. Season with salt and pepper and stir in a handful of pitted black olives. Serve with freshly cooked pasta. **Total cooking time 20 minutes.**

chicken & asparagus calzone

Serves **2**
Total cooking time **30 minutes**

175 g (6 oz) **asparagus
    spears**, trimmed and cut into
    2 cm (1 inch) pieces
145 g (4½ oz) **pizza base mix**
1 **ready-cooked smoked
    chicken breast**, sliced
125 g (4 oz) **Roquefort
    cheese**, crumbled
salt
rocket leaves, to serve

Cook the asparagus in lightly salted boiling water for 3 minutes until just tender, then drain.

Meanwhile, make the pizza base mix according to the packet instructions. Knead lightly until smooth, then roll out thinly to make a large circle, about 30 cm (12 inches) across, then place on a baking sheet.

Scatter the chicken, asparagus and crumbled cheese over half the dough, leaving a 1 cm (½ inch) border. Brush the edges with water, fold the dough over to cover the filling, pressing the edges firmly to seal. Bake in a preheated oven, 220°C (425°F), Gas Mark 7, for 15 minutes until crisp and golden. Serve warm with rocket leaves.

For smoked chicken, asparagus & blue cheese salad, cook 175 g (6 oz) asparagus spears in lightly salted boiling water for 3 minutes until just tender, then drain. Put 150 g (5 oz) mixed salad leaves in a bowl. Add the asparagus, 1 sliced ready-cooked smoked chicken breast and a handful of pine nuts. Drizzle with ready-made blue cheese salad dressing and toss lightly to mix. **Total cooking time 10 minutes.**

chicken souvlaki

Serves **4**
Total cooking time **30 minutes**

3 tablespoons **olive oil**
3 tablespoons **red wine**
1 teaspoon **dried oregano**
finely grated rind and juice of
  1 lemon
1 **garlic clove**, crushed
4 **skinless chicken breast
  fillets**, cut into strips
4 **pitta breads**, warmed and
  split open
salt and **pepper**

To serve
shredded **cabbage**
chopped **cucumber**
chopped **tomato**
chilli sauce

Mix together the olive oil, wine, oregano, lemon rind and juice and garlic in a large bowl. Season with salt and pepper, add the chicken, mix well and leave to marinate for 15 minutes.

Thread the chicken on to metal skewers and place on a foil-lined grill pan. Cook under a preheated hot grill for 8–10 minutes, turning occasionally, until the chicken is cooked and beginning to char at the edges.

Slide the chicken off the skewers into the warm pitta breads and add some shredded cabbage, chopped cucumber, chopped tomato and a dash of chilli sauce.

For hot chicken & hummus pitta pockets, stir-fry 220 g (7½ oz) chicken mini-fillets in 1 tablespoon olive oil with ½ teaspoon dried oregano, 1 teaspoon garlic paste and the grated rind of ½ lemon for 5 minutes until cooked through. Warm 4 pitta breads, cut in half widthways and open out to form pockets. Add the chicken with 4 tablespoons ready-made hummus and crisp cos (romaine) lettuce and serve. **Total cooking time 10 minutes.**

parmesan chicken escalopes

Serves **4**
Total cooking time **20 minutes**

2 **skinless chicken breast
  fillets,** halved horizontally
2 tablespoons **plain flour**
1 **egg,** beaten
125 g (4 oz) **fresh ciabatta
  breadcrumbs**
75 g (3 oz) **Parmesan
  cheese,** freshly grated
3 tablespoons **sunflower oil**
4 small **baguettes,** cut in half
  lengthways
4 tablespoons **mayonnaise**
4 small handfuls of **mixed
  salad leaves**
salt and **pepper**

Place the chicken halves between 2 pieces of clingfilm
and beat with a rolling pin to flatten slightly. Put the
flour on a plate and the egg in a dish. On a separate
plate, mix together the breadcrumbs and Parmesan and
season with salt and pepper.

Coat each piece of chicken lightly in flour, shaking off
any excess, dip into the beaten egg and coat in the
breadcrumb mixture, pressing them on firmly.

Heat the oil in a large frying pan, add the chicken and
cook for about 5 minutes on each side, until golden,
crisp and cooked through.

Fill the baguette pieces with mayonnaise, salad leaves
and the hot chicken.

For chicken Caesar baguettes, stir-fry 2 skinless
chicken breast fillets, cut into strips, in 2 tablespoons
sunflower oil for about 5 minutes or until cooked
through. Pile on to 4 pieces of French bread with mixed
salad leaves and a drizzle of ready-made Caesar salad
dressing. **Total cooking time 10 minutes.**

cheesy chicken omelette

Serves **2**
Total cooking time **10 minutes**

4 eggs
1 tablespoon **cold water**
15 g (½ oz) **butter**
75 g (3 oz) **ready-cooked chicken**, chopped
50 g (2 oz) **Gruyère cheese**, grated
salt and **pepper**
salad, to serve

Put a small nonstick frying pan on the hob to heat. Crack the eggs into a bowl, season with salt and pepper and add the measurement water. Beat with a fork until evenly mixed.

Add the butter to the pan. When it is foaming and melted, pour in the beaten egg mixture. As the eggs begin to set, use a wooden spoon to draw the mixture into the centre of the pan, allowing the runny egg to flow to the edge of the pan.

Cook until the top of the omelette is softly set, then arrange the chicken and cheese down the centre. Starting at the side nearest the handle, flip the omelette over the filling and then tip it out on to a plate. Cut in half and serve with a simple salad.

For chicken & cheese frittata, beat together 4 eggs and season with salt and pepper. Heat 1 tablespoon olive oil in a small frying pan with a heatproof handle. Add 200 g (7 oz) chopped cooked potatoes and fry for 5 minutes until golden. Add 2 chopped spring onions, 75 g (3 oz) chopped ready-cooked chicken and a handful of frozen peas. Heat through, then pour over the eggs. Cook until just set. Arrange 50 g (2 oz) sliced Gruyère on top and cook under a preheated grill until the frittata is just firm and the cheese has melted. **Total cooking time 20 minutes.**

healthy feasts

chicken couscous salad

Serves **4**

Total cooking time **10 minutes**

250 g (8 oz) **couscous**

250 ml (8 fl oz) hot **chicken stock**

400 g (13 oz) can **chickpeas**, drained

200 g (7 oz) **roasted peppers in oil from a jar**, drained and chopped, with 3 tablespoons oil reserved

125 g (4 oz) **cherry tomatoes**, halved

4 tablespoons chopped **mixed herbs**, such as parsley, mint and fresh coriander

200 g (7 oz) **ready-cooked barbecue-flavoured chicken**, chopped

1 tablespoon **white wine vinegar**

1 teaspoon **Dijon mustard**

salt and **pepper**

Put the couscous in a heatproof bowl, pour over the hot stock, cover the bowl with clingfilm and leave to stand for 5–8 minutes until the stock has been absorbed.

Meanwhile, in a large bowl, mix together the chickpeas, peppers, tomatoes, herbs and chicken.

Mix together the oil from the peppers, the vinegar and mustard in a small bowl. Season with salt and pepper. Uncover the couscous, fluff up with a fork, add the dressing and chicken mixture and stir well to mix.

For chicken & couscous stuffed peppers, halve, core and deseed 4 red peppers, then roast in a preheated oven, 220°C (425°F), Gas Mark 7, for 20 minutes until softened and lightly charred. Meanwhile, soak 175 g (6 oz) couscous in 175 ml (6 fl oz) hot chicken stock for 10 minutes or until the stock has been absorbed. Fluff up with a fork and stir in 125 g (4 oz) halved cherry tomatoes, 3 tablespoons chopped mixed parsley, mint and coriander, 175 g (6 oz) chopped ready-cooked barbecue-flavoured chicken and 75 g (3 oz) chopped haloumi cheese. Spoon the mixture into the pepper halves, drizzle with a little olive oil and cook under a preheated grill for 5 minutes to brown. **Total cooking time 30 minutes.**

herby quinoa & chicken

Serves **4**
Total cooking time **30 minutes**

200 g (7 oz) **quinoa**
1 tablespoon **olive oil**
1 **onion**, chopped
1 **garlic clove**, crushed
4 **skinless chicken breast
   fillets**, sliced
1 teaspoon **ground coriander**
½ teaspoon **ground cumin**
50 g (2 oz) **dried cranberries**
75 g (3 oz) **ready-to-eat dried
   apricots**, chopped
4 tablespoons chopped
   parsley
4 tablespoons chopped **mint**
finely grated rind of 1 **lemon**
salt and **pepper**

Cook the quinoa in a pan of lightly salted boiling water for 15 minutes until tender, then drain.

Meanwhile, heat the oil in a large frying pan, add the onion and cook, stirring, for 5 minutes to soften. Add the garlic, chicken, coriander and cumin and cook for a further 8–10 minutes until the chicken is cooked.

Season the quinoa with salt and pepper. Add the chicken mixture, cranberries, apricots, herbs and lemon rind. Stir well and serve warm or cold.

For chicken & apricot Moroccan couscous, put 110 g (3½ oz) Moroccan-flavoured couscous in a heatproof bowl, cover with boiling water, cover the bowl with clingfilm and leave to stand for 8 minutes. When all the water has been absorbed, stir in 250 g (8 oz) chopped ready-cooked chicken, 125 g (4 oz) chopped ready-to-eat apricots and a rinsed and drained 220 g (7½ oz) can chickpeas. **Total cooking time 10 minutes.**

yogurt chicken with greek salad

Serves **4**

Total cooking time **20 minutes**

150 g (5 oz) **fat-free Greek yogurt**

1 **garlic clove**, crushed

2 tablespoons **olive oil**

finely grated rind and juice of 1 **lemon**

1 teaspoon **ground cumin**

4 **skinless chicken breast fillets**, cut into bite-sized chunks

½ **cucumber**, chopped

1 **red onion**, sliced

4 **tomatoes**, cut into slim wedges

16 **pitted black olives**

175 g (6 oz) **feta cheese**, crumbled

1 small **cos (romaine) lettuce**, torn

Dressing

1 tablespoon **lemon juice**

2 tablespoons **olive oil**

1 tablespoon chopped **fresh oregano** or ½ teaspoon **dried oregano**

Soak 8 small wooden skewers in water. In a bowl, mix together the yogurt, garlic, olive oil, lemon rind and juice and cumin. Add the chicken and stir well. Thread on to the skewers and place on a foil-lined grill pan.

Cook under a preheated hot grill for 10 minutes, turning occasionally, or until the chicken is cooked and beginning to char in places.

Meanwhile, in a salad bowl mix together the cucumber, onion, tomatoes, olives, feta and lettuce.

Make the dressing by whisking together the lemon juice, oil and fresh or dried oregano. Pour the dressing over the salad and lightly mix together. Serve with the chicken skewers.

For grilled yogurt chicken & spinach ciabatta,

prepare the chicken skewers as above. Slide the chicken off the skewers. Split a ciabatta loaf lengthways and spread the bottom half with mayonnaise. Top with a handful of baby spinach leaves, a few teaspoons of tomato chilli jam and the hot chicken. Cover with the top half of the ciabatta loaf, then cut into 4 to serve. **Total cooking time 15 minutes.**

chicken pasta salad with pesto

Serves **4**
Total cooking time **20 minutes**

2 **boneless, skinless chicken breasts**
½ tablespoon **olive oil**
150 g (5 oz) **conchiglie pasta**
4 tablespoons **walnut halves**
1 small **red onion**, sliced
225 g (7½ oz) **baby plum tomatoes**, halved
½ **cucumber**, cut into chunks
100 g (3½ oz) **watercress**
2 tablespoons **Parmesan cheese shavings**, to serve

Dressing
1½ tablespoons **olive oil**
2 tablespoons **ready-made pesto**
1 tablespoon **balsamic vinegar**

Make the pesto dressing by whisking together all the ingredients in a small bowl and set aside.

Brush the chicken breasts with the oil, then cook in a preheated hot griddle pan for 12–15 minutes, turning once, until cooked through.

Meanwhile, cook the pasta in a saucepan of boiling water for 8–9 minutes, or according to the packet instructions, until 'al dente'. Drain, then refresh under cold running water and drain again.

Heat a nonstick frying pan over a medium-low heat and dry-fry the walnuts for 3–4 minutes, stirring frequently, until slightly golden.

Cut the chicken into thin slices, then place in a large bowl with the pasta, toasted walnuts, onion, tomatoes, cucumber and watercress.

Toss with the pesto dressing and serve sprinkled with the Parmesan cheese shavings.

For chicken pesto baguettes, halve 4 baguettes horizontally and spread the bases of each with ½ tablespoon ready-made pesto. Divide 50 g (2 oz) watercress between the baguettes and top with 4 sliced tomatoes, ¼ sliced cucumber, ½ sliced red onion and 2 sliced ready-cooked chicken breasts. Top each with a dollop of mayonnaise, then replace the tops. **Total cooking time 10 minutes.**

coronation chicken with avocado

Serves **4**
Total cooking time **10 minutes**

150 g (5 oz) **mayonnaise**
1½ teaspoons **mild curry powder**
1 teaspoon **ground allspice**
1 **red chilli**, deseeded and diced
juice of ½ **lime**
6 tablespoons **mango chutney**
6 tablespoons **Greek yogurt**
550 g (1 lb 2 oz) **ready-cooked chicken**, shredded
½ **iceberg lettuce**, leaves torn
30 g (1 oz) **watercress**
2 **avocados**, stoned, peeled and sliced
2 large **beef tomatoes**, sliced
2 tablespoons **toasted flaked almonds**

Mix together the mayonnaise, curry powder, allspice, chilli, lime juice, chutney and yogurt in a large bowl, then stir in the chicken.

Place the lettuce on a serving plate, then top with the watercress, avocados and tomatoes.

Spoon over the chicken and serve sprinkled with the almonds.

For chicken kebabs with avocado dip, put 2 garlic cloves, 1 tablespoon grated fresh root ginger and 3 chopped spring onions in a pestle and mortar and grind to a paste. Stir in the juice of ½ lime, 1 tablespoon soy sauce and 1 tablespoon vegetable oil. Place 625 g (1¼ lb) cubed skinless chicken breast fillets and 20 button mushrooms in a bowl, pour over the marinade and toss. Thread the chicken, mushrooms and 20 cherry tomatoes on to 16 metal skewers. Cook in a preheated hot griddle pan for 7–8 minutes on each side until cooked through. Meanwhile, mix together 2 stoned, peeled and mashed avocados, the juice of ½ lemon, 2 chopped tomatoes and a pinch of chilli flakes. Serve with the kebabs. **Total cooking time 30 minutes.**

chicken liver salad

Serves **4**

Total cooking time **10 minutes**

200 g (7 oz) **streaky bacon rashers**

5 tablespoons **olive oil**

200 g (7 oz) **crusty bread**, cut into small cubes

400 g (13 oz) **chicken livers**, halved and trimmed

25 g (1 oz) **watercress**

50 g (2 oz) **lamb's lettuce**

3 small **ready-cooked fresh beetroot**, cut into wedges

1 **red onion**, sliced

1 tablespoon **raspberry vinegar**

1 tablespoon **Dijon mustard**

1 teaspoon **clear honey**

Cook the bacon under a preheated hot grill for 6–8 minutes until crisp.

Meanwhile, heat 1 tablespoon of the oil in a frying pan, add the bread and cook for 3–4 minutes, turning frequently, until golden. Remove from the pan with a slotted spoon and drain on kitchen paper.

Heat another tablespoon of the oil in the pan and cook the chicken livers for 2–3 minutes on each side until golden brown but still slightly pink in the middle. Leave to cool slightly, then cut into bite-sized pieces.

Toss together the watercress, lamb's lettuce, beetroot and onion in a serving bowl, then add the chicken livers and croutons. Top with the bacon.

Whisk together the remaining oil, vinegar, mustard and honey in a small bowl and drizzle over the salad to serve.

For chicken liver & mustard pâté, melt 100 g (3½ oz) butter in a frying pan over a medium heat, add 1 diced onion and cook for 3–4 minutes. Add 1 crushed garlic clove and 450 g (14½ oz) trimmed and halved chicken livers and fry for 6–8 minutes until cooked through. Stir in 1 tablespoon brandy and 1 teaspoon mustard powder and season well. Tip into a food processor with 65 g (2½ oz) melted butter and blitz until smooth. Pour into 4 small ramekins and leave to cool before serving. **Total cooking time 20 minutes.**

citrus chicken salad

Serves **2**
Total cooking time **10 minutes**

1 **orange**
4 **ready-cooked roast chicken thighs**
75 g (3 oz) **watercress**
1 **avocado**, stoned, peeled and sliced
2 teaspoons **walnut** or **olive oil**
shelled walnut pieces (optional)

Place the orange on a chopping board and use a small sharp knife to cut off the top and bottom so that you cut right through the peel and outside pith to the flesh. Now cut the remaining peel and pith away from the flesh, cutting in strips downwards, following the curve of the orange. Cut the orange into fleshy segments, using a sharp knife to carefully cut either side of the inside pith. Discard the peel and pith, keeping only the segments.

Slice or shred the cooked chicken thighs, discarding the bones and skin, if preferred. Divide the watercress between 2 plates and arrange the orange segments, chicken and sliced avocado attractively over the watercress. Drizzle with walnut oil and scatter over a few walnut pieces, if liked.

For citrus baked chicken, wrap 4 rindless streaky bacon rashers around 2 boneless, skinless chicken breasts and pan-fry in 1 tablespoon olive oil over a medium-high heat for 2 minutes on each side until golden. Meanwhile, warm 200 ml (7 fl oz) orange juice in a pan with ½ teaspoon dried thyme and 2 teaspoons wholegrain mustard. Put the chicken in an ovenproof dish, pour over the juice and bake in a preheated oven, 200°C (400°F), Gas Mark 6, for about 20 minutes until the chicken is cooked through. Slice thickly, arrange on 2 warmed plates, drizzle over the orangey juices and serve with a watercress and avocado salad. **Total cooking time 30 minutes.**

chicken tacos

Serves **4**
Total cooking time **20 minutes**

1 tablespoon **vegetable oil**
500 g (1 lb) **minced chicken**
2 **garlic cloves**, crushed
30 g (1½ oz) **taco** or **fajita**
   seasoning mix
juice of **1 lime**
8 **taco shells**

To serve
tomato salsa
shredded **crisp lettuce**
Greek yogurt
lime wedges

Heat the oil in a frying pan, add the minced chicken and stir-fry, keeping the meat in clumps. Add the garlic and seasoning mix and continue cooking for 5 minutes, adding a little water if the mixture becomes too dry. Stir in the lime juice.

Warm the taco shells according to the packet instructions. Spoon in the mince mixture and top with tomato salsa and shredded lettuce. Serve with lime wedges and yogurt on the side.

For Tex–Mex chicken & beans, fry 500 g (1 lb) minced chicken in 1 tablespoon sunflower oil over a high heat with 30 g (1½ oz) taco or fajita seasoning mix for 5 minutes until clumpy and cooked. Add 250 ml (8 fl oz) passata and a rinsed and drained 220 g (7½ oz) can kidney beans. Heat through and serve on thick slices of toast from a crusty loaf. **Total cooking time 10 minutes.**

chicken dippers with hummus

Serves **4**

Total cooking time **10 minutes**

1 tablespoon **plain flour**

1 tablespoon chopped **parsley**

1 tablespoon chopped **fresh coriander**

300 g (10 oz) **chicken mini-fillets**

25 g (1 oz) **butter**

1 tablespoon **olive oil**

Hummus

1 **garlic clove**, finely diced

400 g (13 oz) can **chickpeas**, rinsed and drained

juice of ½ **lemon**

2 tablespoons **tahini paste**

3–4 tablespoons **extra virgin olive oil**

Mix together the flour and herbs on a plate, then toss the chicken strips in the herbed flour.

Heat the butter and olive oil in a large frying pan, add the chicken and cook for 3–4 minutes on each side or until golden and cooked through.

Meanwhile, make the hummus. Place the garlic, chickpeas, lemon juice and tahini in a food processor or blender and blend until nearly smooth. With the motor still running, pour in the extra virgin olive oil through the feed tube and blend to the desired consistency.

Serve the chicken with hummus for dipping.

For spiced chicken breasts with hummus, mix together 1 crushed garlic clove and ½ tablespoon each of paprika, dried thyme, cayenne pepper and ground black pepper in a small bowl, then rub over 4 boneless, skinless chicken breasts, about 150 g (5 oz) each. Cook the chicken breasts under a preheated hot grill for 6–8 minutes on each side or until cooked through. Spoon 300 g (10 oz) ready-made hummus into a bowl. Serve the chicken with the hummus and a rocket salad. **Total cooking time 20 minutes.**

nectarine-glazed chicken kebabs

Serves **4**
Total cooking time **30 minutes**

2 **nectarines**, halved, stoned and roughly chopped
4 cm (1½ inch) piece of **fresh root ginger,** peeled and roughly chopped
2 **garlic cloves**, chopped
1 teaspoon **soy sauce**
1 teaspoon **Worcestershire sauce**
2 teaspoons **olive oil**
600 g (1 lb 5 oz) **skinless chicken breast fillets,** cut into bite-sized pieces
1 **red pepper**, cored, deseeded and cut into bite-sized pieces
1 **yellow pepper**, cored, deseeded and cut into bite-sized pieces
crisp green salad, to serve

Place the nectarines, ginger, garlic, soy sauce, Worcestershire sauce and oil in a small food processor or blender and blitz until completely smooth.

Put the chicken and peppers in a nonreactive bowl and pour over the marinade. Cover and leave to marinate in the refrigerator for 5 minutes.

Thread the pieces of chicken and pepper on to metal skewers and cook under a preheated medium grill or on the barbecue for 12–15 minutes, turning frequently, or until the chicken is cooked through.

Serve with a crisp green salad.

For chicken & nectarine salad, whisk together 1 tablespoon white wine vinegar, 3 tablespoons olive oil, 1 tablespoon chopped mint, 1 teaspoon clear honey and ½ teaspoon Dijon mustard in a bowl. Toss together 3 halved, stoned and sliced nectarines, 400 g (13 oz) cubed ready-cooked chicken breasts, 1 chopped cucumber, ½ sliced red onion and 50 g (2 oz) rocket leaves in a serving bowl. Toss with the dressing and serve with crusty bread. **Total cooking time 10 minutes**.

grilled tandoori chicken skewers

Serves **4**
Total cooking time **30 minutes**

175 g (6 oz) **fat-free Greek
  yogurt**, plus extra to serve
2 tablespoons **tandoori paste**
500 g (1 lb) **skinless chicken
  breast fillets**, cut into strips
2 teaspoons **cumin seeds**
1 **small cucumber**
½ **red onion**, cut in half and
  finely sliced
3 tablespoons **fresh coriander
  leaves**
2 **lemons**, cut into wedges
salt and **pepper**
mini naan breads, to serve
  (optional)

Mix together the yogurt and tandoori paste in a large
bowl, add the chicken and toss until the chicken is well
coated. Set aside to marinate for 10 minutes.

Heat a small nonstick frying pan over a medium heat,
add the cumin seeds and dry-fry for 1–2 minutes,
stirring frequently. Remove from the heat when the
seeds become fragrant and begin to smoke.

Thread the chicken strips on to 8 small metal skewers
and lay on a foil-lined baking sheet. Cook under a
preheated hot grill for 8–10 minutes, turning once,
until the chicken is cooked through.

Meanwhile, slice the cucumber into ribbons using a
sharp vegetable peeler and arrange on 4 serving plates.
Scatter the onion and coriander over the cucumber,
sprinkle over the toasted cumin seeds and season lightly
with salt and pepper. Place the chicken skewers and
lemon wedges on top. Serve immediately with warm
naan breads and extra yogurt.

For tandoori chicken & salad naans, stir together
1 teaspoon tandoori paste and 6 tablespoons fat-free
natural yogurt in a bowl. Roughly slice 300 g (10 oz)
ready-cooked chicken breast and mix with the tandoori
yogurt. Cut ½ cucumber into ribbons, using a vegetable
peeler, and finely slice ½ red onion. Divide the chicken
into 4 mini naan breads, then divide the cucumber,
onion, ½ teaspoon cumin seeds and a few coriander
leaves into the naans. Squeeze a little lemon juice over
the salad and serve immediately. **Total cooking time
10 minutes.**

chinese chicken wraps

Serves **4**
Total cooking time **10 minutes**

4 large **tortilla wraps**
4 tablespoons **plum sauce**,
  plus extra to serve (optional)
300 g (10 oz) **ready-cooked**
  chicken breasts, such as
  sweet chilli cooked chicken,
  sliced
½ **cucumber**, cut into batons
3 **spring onions**, finely sliced
  lengthways
1 large **cos (romaine) lettuce**
  heart, shredded

Spread the tortilla wraps with the plum sauce, then top each wrap with the chicken, cucumber and spring onions. Finish with the lettuce and roll up tightly.

Cut in half diagonally and serve with a little extra plum sauce, if liked.

For chicken filo pastries with plum sauce, mix together in a bowl 400 g (13 oz) shredded ready-cooked chicken, 3 finely sliced spring onions, 1 grated carrot, 100 g (3½ oz) finely shredded mangetout and 1 finely chopped small bunch of coriander until combined. Cut 8 sheets of filo pastry to 15 x 25 cm (6 x 10 inches). Put one-eighth of the chicken mixture along the end of one rectangle, leaving a gap at the edge. Fold in the longer pastry sides, then roll up into a cigar shape. Brush with melted butter to seal and repeat to make 8 pastries. Place on a lightly greased baking sheet and cook in a preheated oven, 200°C (400°F), Gas Mark 6, for 18–20 minutes until golden and crisp. Serve with plum sauce. **Total cooking time 30 minutes.**

chicken with coriander aïoli

Serves **4**
Total cooking time **20 minutes**

2 teaspoons coarsely crushed
  black peppercorns
4 **skinless chicken breast**
  fillets, thinly sliced
1 tablespoon **olive oil**

Coriander aïoli
small bunch of **fresh**
  coriander, leaves only
1 **garlic clove**, peeled
2 teaspoons **Dijon mustard**
1 **egg yolk**
2 teaspoons **white wine**
  vinegar
150 ml (¼ pint) **sunflower oil**
salt and **pepper**

To serve
green salad
grated **beetroot**

Make the coriander aioli. Reserve a few coriander leaves for garnish and place the rest in a small food processor or blender with the garlic, mustard, egg yolk and vinegar. Blend until finely chopped. With the motor still running, slowly drizzle in the sunflower oil through the feed tube until the mixture is smooth and thick. Season with salt and pepper.

Scatter the crushed peppercorns over the chicken slices and drizzle with the olive oil. Cook, in batches, on a preheated hot griddle for 1–2 minutes on each side or until cooked through and golden.

Serve the warm chicken slices with mixed green salad leaves, grated beetroot and the coriander aïoli. Garnish with the reserved coriander leaves.

For griddled chicken & tomato sandwiches, thinly slice 3 skinless chicken breast fillets, season with salt and plenty of pepper and drizzle with 1 tablespoon olive oil. Cut 4 tomatoes in half, season and drizzle with a little oil. Cook the chicken and tomatoes, in batches, on a preheated hot griddle for 1–2 minutes on each side until cooked and golden. Sandwich between slices of crusty granary bread with rocket leaves and ready-made roast garlic mayonnaise. **Total cooking time 10 minutes.**

saucy lemon chicken with greens

Serves **4**

Total cooking time **30 minutes**

2 teaspoons **sesame oil**

4 **skinless, boneless chicken breasts**

1 **red chilli**, deseeded and chopped

finely grated rind of **1 lemon**

8 tablespoons **lemon juice**

2 **pak choi**, halved

1 tablespoon **cornflour**, mixed to a paste with 2 tablespoons water

Heat the sesame oil in a large, heavy-based frying pan, add the chicken breasts and fry for 5 minutes, turning once, or until browned. Add the chilli to the pan with the lemon rind and juice. Cover and simmer for 15 minutes or until the chicken is cooked through.

Meanwhile, steam or lightly cook the pak choi in a little lightly salted boiling water until just tender.

Remove the chicken from the pan and keep warm. Stir the cornflour paste into the pan juices and bring to the boil, stirring until thickened and adding a little water if the sauce is too thick. Serve the chicken with the pak choi and the lemon sauce poured over the top.

For lemon noodle chicken, stir-fry 200 g (7 oz) chicken mini-fillets in 2 teaspoons sesame oil for 5 minutes or until browned and cooked through. Add 75 g (3 oz) lemon stir-fry sauce, 300 g (10 oz) ready-prepared mixed stir-fry vegetables and 150 g (5 oz) ready-cooked noodles. Cook, stirring, for 5 minutes, then serve. **Total cooking time 10 minutes.**

chicken & apricot stew

Serves **4**

Total cooking time **30 minutes**

1 tablespoon **olive oil**

2 **garlic cloves**, crushed

1 tablespoon peeled and
grated **fresh root ginger**

1 large **onion**, chopped

600 g (1 lb 5 oz) **chicken
breast fillets**, cubed

100 g (3½ oz) **red split lentils**

1 teaspoon **ground cumin**

¼ teaspoon **ground
cinnamon**

¼ teaspoon **ground turmeric**

¼ teaspoon **ground coriander**

12 **ready-to-eat dried
apricots**

juice of 1 **lemon**

750 ml (1¼ pints) hot **chicken
stock**

1 tablespoon chopped **mint**

1 tablespoon chopped **fresh
coriander**

seeds of 1 **pomegranate**

2 tablespoons **toasted flaked
almonds**

couscous, to serve

Heat the oil in a large saucepan, add the garlic, ginger and onion and cook for 1–2 minutes. Add the chicken and cook for a further 5 minutes, stirring occasionally.

Add the lentils, spices, apricots and lemon juice and stir well. Pour in the stock and bring to the boil, then reduce the heat and simmer for 15 minutes until the chicken is cooked through.

Stir in the herbs and pomegranate seeds, then sprinkle with the almonds. Serve in bowls with couscous.

For chicken & apricot wraps, spread 4 tortilla wraps with 2 tablespoons mayonnaise. Top each with the leaves of ½ Little Gem lettuce, ½ cored, deseeded and sliced red pepper, 2 chopped ready-to-eat dried apricots, a few coriander leaves, 100 g (3½ oz) diced ready-cooked chicken breasts and 2 teaspoons mango chutney. Roll up the wraps and serve. **Total cooking time 10 minutes.**

honey-mustard chicken with slaw

Serves **4**

Total cooking time **20 minutes**

3 tablespoons **clear honey**

2 tablespoons **wholegrain mustard**

1 tablespoon **Worcestershire sauce**

1 tablespoon **dark soy sauce**

625 g (1 ¼ lb) **chicken mini-fillets**

mixed leaf salad, to serve

Coleslaw

½ **red cabbage**, shredded

½ small **red onion**, thinly sliced

1 large **carrot**, coarsely grated

4–6 tablespoons **ready-made Caesar dressing**

Put the honey, mustard, Worcestershire sauce and soy sauce in a large bowl and mix to combine. Tip in the chicken fillets and toss until the chicken is well coated in the glaze.

Scrape the chicken into a foil-lined roasting tin, spread out over the base and then place in a preheated oven, 200°C (400°F), Gas Mark 6, for about 15 minutes, turning once, until cooked through.

Meanwhile, make the coleslaw. Combine the cabbage, red onion and carrot in a large bowl, then mix with 4–6 tablespoons of the Caesar dressing, depending on the consistency desired.

Serve the glazed fillets on top of a mixed leaf salad together with the coleslaw.

For honey & mustard chicken slaw salad, make a honey and mustard dressing by combining 1 tablespoon honey, 1 tablespoon wholegrain mustard, 1½ tablespoons Worcestershire sauce, 2 teaspoons dark soy sauce and 2–3 tablespoons freshly squeezed orange juice in a jug or bowl. In a large bowl, toss together 400 g (13 oz) ready-cooked chicken mini-fillets, ½ shredded red cabbage, ½ thinly sliced small red onion and 1 coarsely grated large carrot. Arrange the chicken and cabbage salad on serving plates, scatter with 150 g (5 oz) ready-made croutons and drizzle over the dressing. Serve immediately. **Total cooking time 10 minutes.**

chicken & aubergine bake

Serves **4**
Total cooking time **30 minutes**

1 **aubergine**, thinly sliced
olive oil spray
6 **skinless chicken thigh
   fillets**, chopped
350 g (11½ oz) **ready-made
   tomato and basil pasta
   sauce**
150 g (5 oz) **mozzarella
   cheese**, chopped
50 g (2 oz) **fresh white
   breadcrumbs**
2 tablespoons grated
   Parmesan cheese
salt and **pepper**

Place the aubergine slices on a foil-lined grill pan and lightly spray with oil. Cook under a preheated grill for about 5 minutes, turning once, or until tender.

Meanwhile, lightly spray a nonstick frying pan with oil, add the chicken and cook over a high heat for 5 minutes or until cooked through. Stir in the pasta sauce and bring to the boil.

Place half the aubergine slices in the base of an ovenproof dish, pour the chicken and tomato mixture over the top and cover with the remaining aubergine. Mix together the mozzarella, breadcrumbs, Parmesan and seasoning and sprinkle over the top. Bake in a preheated oven, 200°C (400°F), Gas Mark 6, for 15 minutes until the topping is golden and crisp.

For chicken, aubergine & tomato soup, stir-fry 4 chopped skinless chicken thigh fillets in 1 tablespoon olive oil with 1 chopped aubergine for 5 minutes or until cooked through. Stir in 600 ml (1 pint) ready-made tomato soup and heat through until hot. Serve with a swirl of low-fat yogurt. **Total cooking time 10 minutes.**

chicken with orange & olives

Serves **4**

Total cooking time **30 minutes**

2 tablespoons **olive oil**

4 **boneless, skinless chicken breasts**, about 150 g (5 oz) each

750 ml (1¼ pints) **chicken stock**

a few **thyme sprigs**

12 **black olives**, pitted

2 **oranges**, segmented

225 g (7½ oz) **bulgar wheat**

3 tablespoons **toasted flaked almonds**

2 tablespoons chopped **parsley**

salt and **pepper**

Heat the oil in a large frying pan, add the chicken and cook for 3–4 minutes on each side until browned. Pour in 450 ml (¾ pint) of the stock, then stir in the thyme, olives and orange segments. Cover and simmer for 15–16 minutes until cooked through.

Meanwhile, place the bulgar wheat in a saucepan with the remaining stock, season to taste and simmer for 8–10 minutes until most of the water is absorbed. Remove the pan from the heat and stir in the almonds, then cover and leave to stand.

Remove the chicken from the frying pan and keep warm. Simmer the sauce for 4–5 minutes until reduced by half. Stir in the chopped parsley.

Serve the chicken with the bulgar wheat, drizzled with the thyme, olive and orange sauce.

For chicken, orange & olive sandwiches, toast 8 slices of wholemeal bread under a preheated hot grill for 2–3 minutes on each side. Spread 4 of the slices with 2 teaspoons ready-made pesto each, then top each with a small handful of bistro salad leaves, a few orange segments, 2–3 slices of ready-cooked chicken, 1 sliced tomato and 2–3 sliced pitted olives. Top with the remaining toast and serve. **Total cooking time 10 minutes.**

sweet chilli chicken stir-fry

Serves **4**

Total cooking time **20 minutes**

1 tablespoon **groundnut oil**

500 g (1 lb) **skinless chicken breast fillets**, cut into bite-sized pieces

1 large **onion**, cut into large pieces

2 **garlic cloves**, sliced

1 tablespoon peeled and finely chopped **fresh root ginger**

100 g (3½ oz) **pineapple**, peeled and 'eyes' removed, sliced and cut into wedges

250 g (8 oz) **sweet chilli stir-fry sauce**

150 g (5 oz) **water chestnuts**, halved

1 tablespoon **soy sauce**

1 tablespoon **lime juice**

125 g (4 oz) **frozen peas**

2 tablespoons roughly chopped **unsalted cashew nuts**

steamed **rice**, to serve

Heat the oil in a wok or large frying pan over a medium heat. Tip in the chicken pieces and cook for 3–4 minutes, stirring frequently, until golden brown all over. Remove from the heat with a slotted spoon and set aside.

Add the onion to the wok and stir-fry for 2–3 minutes until golden and beginning to soften, then add the garlic and ginger and stir-fry for 1–2 minutes. Stir in the pineapple and sweet chilli sauce, then bring to the boil.

Return the chicken to the pan with the water chestnuts, soy sauce and lime juice and stir to combine. Reduce the heat and simmer gently for 4–6 minutes until the chicken is cooked through, then add the peas and stir for 1–2 minutes until hot. Scatter over the cashew nuts and serve immediately with steamed rice.

For quick sweet chilli chicken stir-fry, heat
2 teaspoons groundnut oil in a large frying pan. Add 1 teaspoon each of finely chopped garlic and fresh root ginger. Stir-fry for 30 seconds. Add 400 g (13 oz) ready-prepared stir-fry vegetables and fry for 3–4 minutes, then add 400 g (13 oz) ready-cooked chicken slices, 100 g (3½ oz) pineapple, cut into bite-sized wedges, 250 g (8 oz) sweet chilli stir-fry sauce, 1 tablespoon soy sauce and 1 tablespoon lime juice. Stir until hot, then spoon into deep bowls over 500 g (1 lb) hot ready-cooked rice. **Total cooking time 10 minutes.**

mild & creamy chicken curry

Serves **4**
Total cooking time **30 minutes**

1½ tablespoons **groundnut oil**

1 large **onion**, sliced

2 **garlic cloves**, finely chopped

1 teaspoon **ground turmeric**

1 teaspoon **ground cumin**

1 teaspoon **ground coriander**

150 g (5 oz) **korma paste**

500 g (1 lb) **skinless chicken breast fillets**, cubed

250 g (8 oz) **sweet potatoes**, peeled and cubed

200 ml (7 fl oz) **coconut milk**

100 ml (3½ fl oz) **water**

2 tablespoons **ground almonds**

250 g (8 oz) **basmati rice**, rinsed

salt and **pepper**

fresh coriander, to garnish

naan bread, to serve

Heat the oil in a saucepan or deep frying pan over a medium heat, add the onion and cook for 5–6 minutes, stirring frequently, until softened.

Add the garlic, spices and korma paste and stir-fry for 1–2 minutes, then stir in the chicken and sweet potatoes. Cook for 3–4 minutes to seal the chicken, then add the coconut milk, water and ground almonds and season with salt and pepper. Bring to the boil, then reduce the heat and simmer gently for 12–15 minutes until the chicken is cooked through and the potato is tender.

Meanwhile, put the basmati rice in a large pan of lightly salted boiling water and cook for 12 minutes until tender, or according to the packet instructions.

Serve the curry on a bed of rice, garnished with the coriander and with naan bread on the side, if liked.

For grilled korma chicken with rice, cut 3–4 deep slashes in 4 boneless, skinless chicken breasts, about 150 g (5 oz) each, then cover each breast with 1 tablespoon korma paste. Place the chicken on a foil-lined baking sheet and cook under a preheated hot grill for 12–15 minutes, turning once, until cooked. Serve with 500 g (1 lb) ready-cooked basmati rice, topped with a couple of dollops natural yogurt and with lemon wedges on the side. **Total cooking time 20 minutes.**

chicken pilau with cauliflower

Serves **4**
Total cooking time **30 minutes**

1 tablespoon **sunflower oil**
1 **onion**, chopped
6 **skinless chicken thigh
  fillets**, chopped
2 tablespoons **korma curry
  paste**
250 ml (8 fl oz) **basmati rice**
  (measured in a measuring
  jug)
1 litre (1¾ pints) **chicken
  stock**
1 small **cauliflower**, cut into
  florets
125 g (4 oz) **green beans**,
  trimmed and halved
  widthways
2 **carrots**, coarsely grated
25 g (1 oz) **toasted flaked
  almonds**
salt and **pepper**
low-fat natural yogurt, to
  serve

Heat the oil in a large pan, add the onion and chicken
and cook, stirring, for 5 minutes. Stir in the curry paste,
rice, stock, cauliflower and green beans. Bring to the
boil, reduce the heat, cover and simmer for 10 minutes
until the stock has been absorbed, the rice and
vegetables are tender and the chicken is cooked through.

Stir in the grated carrot, heat through for 1 minute,
and season with salt and pepper. Sprinkle with flaked
almonds and serve with natural yogurt.

For curried chicken with vegetable rice, heat
2 tablespoons korma paste in a pan, add 200 g (7 oz)
chopped ready-cooked chicken, 200 g (7 oz) frozen
mixed vegetables and about 4 tablespoons boiling
water. Cover and cook for 5 minutes, then stir in
500 g (1 lb) ready-cooked pilau rice and heat through,
stirring, for 3 minutes, until hot. **Total cooking time
10 minutes.**

chicken & vegetable stir-fry

Serves **4**
Total cooking time **15 minutes**

2 tablespoons **coconut oil**
3cm (1¼ inch) piece of **fresh
    root ginger**, peeled and
    finely diced
2 **garlic cloves**, crushed
1 **onion**, chopped
450 g (14½ oz) **skinless
    chicken breast fillets**, cut
    into strips
125 g (4 oz) **mushrooms**,
    quartered
300 g (10 oz) **broccoli florets**
125 g (4 oz) **curly kale**,
    chopped
1–2 tablespoons **soy sauce**
2 tablespoons **sesame seeds**

Heat the oil in a wok or large frying pan until hot, add
the ginger, garlic and onion and stir-fry for 30 seconds.
Add the chicken and stir-fry for a further 2–3 minutes.

Add the vegetables, then sprinkle over the soy sauce.
Stir-fry for 1–2 minutes, then cover and steam for a
further 4–5 minutes until the vegetables are tender
and the chicken is cooked through.

Serve sprinkled with the sesame seeds.

For chicken & oriental vegetable stir-fry, heat
2 tablespoons coconut oil in a wok until hot, add
6 chopped spring onions, 2 crushed garlic cloves and
1 tablespoon peeled and grated fresh root ginger
and stir-fry for 2 minutes. Add 450 g (14½ oz) sliced
chicken breast fillets, and stir-fry for 2–3 minutes. Add
75 g (3 oz) baby sweetcorn and 1 cored, deseeded and
sliced red pepper and stir-fry for a further 3–4 minutes.
Stir in 100 g (3½ oz) chopped shiitake mushrooms,
50 g (2 oz) bean sprouts and 2 chopped pak choi and
stir-fry for 4–5 minutes. Stir in 2 tablespoons oyster
sauce and 1 teaspoon soy sauce and cook for a further
4–5 minutes. Serve sprinkled with 2 tablespoons
toasted sesame seeds. **Total cooking time 20 minutes.**

moroccan fruity chicken stew

Serves **4**

Total cooking time **30 minutes**

1 tablespoon **olive oil**

1 large **red onion**, cut in large
chunks

1 **onion**, cut into large chunks

375 g (12 oz) **skinless
chicken breast fillets**, diced

1 teaspoon **ground cumin**

1 teaspoon **paprika**

1 teaspoon **ground coriander**

½ teaspoon **ground
cinnamon**

½ teaspoon **ground ginger**

125 g (4 oz) **dried prunes**

125 g (4 oz) **ready-to-eat
dried apricots**

400 g (13 oz) can **chickpeas**

600 ml (1 pint) **rich chicken
stock**

1 tablespoon **cornflour**, mixed
to a paste with
2 tablespoons water

4 tablespoons chopped **fresh
coriander**

Heat the oil in a large, heavy-based saucepan, add the
onions and chicken and cook over a medium-high heat
for 10 minutes, stirring occasionally, or until golden in
places and soft. Add the spices, stir and cook for a
further 2 minutes to help the flavours infuse.

Stir in the prunes and apricots, chickpeas and stock and
bring to the boil. Cover and cook for 15 minutes until all
the ingredients are soft and cooked through.

Add the cornflour paste and stir well to thicken slightly,
then stir in the fresh coriander. Serve with couscous,
if liked.

For Moroccan chicken & bean soup, heat
1 tablespoon olive oil in a saucepan and add 1 thinly
sliced red onion and 250 g (8 oz) thinly sliced chicken
breast fillets and cook for 3–4 minutes. Add 1 teaspoon
ground cumin, 1 teaspoon ground coriander and
½ teaspoon ground cinnamon and cook for 30 seconds.
Pour in 600 ml (1 pint) chicken stock and a drained
400 g (13 oz) can chickpeas. Bring to the boil, then
reduce the heat and add 50 g (2 oz) roughly chopped
dried prunes. Cook for a further 4 minutes until piping
hot and the chicken is cooked through. Process in a
blender for a smooth soup, if liked. **Total cooking time
10 minutes.**

chicken & prawn spring rolls

Serves **4**

Total cooking time **30 minutes**

200 g (7 oz) ready-**prepared
   mixed stir-fry vegetables**
1 tablespoon **sesame oil**
1 **red chilli**, deseeded and
   chopped
1 cm (½ inch) piece of **fresh
   root ginger**, peeled and
   grated
200 g (7 oz) **ready-cooked
   chicken**, chopped
125 g (4 oz) small **peeled
   prawns**, thawed if frozen,
   chopped
2 tablespoons **Chinese stir-
   fry sauce**, any flavour
6 sheets **filo pastry**
2 tablespoons **sunflower oil**
salt and **pepper**
teriyaki sauce, for dipping

Chop the stir-fry vegetables to make the pieces slightly smaller, then place in a bowl. Add the sesame oil, chilli, ginger, chicken, prawns and sauce. Season with salt and pepper and mix well.

Work with 1 sheet of filo pastry at a time and keep the rest covered with clingfilm to prevent it from drying out. Cut each sheet in half widthways and put one-twelfth of the chicken mixture at one end of each strip. Roll it up, tucking in the ends as you roll. Place on a baking sheet and brush with a little sunflower oil. Repeat with remaining pastry and filling to make 12 rolls.

Bake in a preheated oven, 200°C (400°F), Gas Mark 6, for 15 minutes until golden and crisp. Serve warm with teriyaki sauce for dipping.

For teriyaki chicken rolls, warm 12 pancakes (the sort used for crispy duck) in the microwave according to the packet instructions. Fill with 250 g (8 oz) ready-cooked chicken, cut into strips, 6 spring onions, cut into fine strips, and ¼ cucumber, cut into sticks. Top with a little teriyaki sauce, roll up and serve. **Total cooking time 10 minutes.**

chicken parcels with mozzarella

Serves **4**
Total cooking time **30 minutes**

4 **skinless, boneless chicken
  breasts**, about 150 g (5 oz)
  each
4 teaspoons **ready-made red
  chilli pesto** or **mild harissa**
2 **plum tomatoes**, sliced
125 g (4 oz) **mozzarella
  cheese**, cut into 8 slices
1 small bunch of **basil**, leaves
  stripped
8 thin slices of **chorizo**

To serve
500 g (1 lb) **ready-made
  healthy couscous** or bulgar
  wheat salad
rocket leaves

Place the chicken breasts between 2 large sheets of
clingfilm on a chopping board and beat with a rolling
pin to flatten; they need to be about 4–5 mm (¼ inch)
thick. Spread 1 teaspoon of the pesto or mild harissa
evenly over each flattened chicken breast.

Cover half of each chicken breast with 2–3 slices
of tomato and 2 slices of mozzarella, then fold the
uncovered half of the chicken over the filling to create
a sandwich. Scatter the basil leaves over the top of the
chicken parcels, reserving a few to garnish.

Cover each parcel with 2 thin slices of the chorizo,
then secure with a wooden cocktail stick by threading
it through the chicken breast. Place the parcels on a
large, nonstick baking sheet, then cook in a preheated
oven, 220°C (425°F), Gas Mark 7, for 15–18 minutes
or until cooked through.

Serve the chicken parcels with the couscous or bulgar
wheat salad and rocket leaves, garnished with the
reserved basil leaves.

For chicken & tomato salad with pesto dressing,
slice 400 g (13 oz) ready-cooked chicken breast and
arrange on serving plates with 150 g (5 oz) rocket
leaves and 200 g (7 oz) halved cherry tomatoes. Top
with 2 tablespoons Parmesan cheese shavings. Whisk
2 tablespoons pesto into 3 tablespoons aged balsamic
vinegar and drizzle over the salad. Serve with warmed,
sliced flatbreads. **Total cooking time 10 minutes.**

crispy stuffed chicken breasts

Serves **4**
Total cooking time **30 minutes**

4 **skinless, boneless chicken breasts**, about 150 g (5 oz) each
100 g (3½ oz) **cream cheese**
1 large **garlic clove**, finely chopped
2 tablespoons chopped **parsley**
½ tablespoon **lemon juice**
1 teaspoon finely grated **lemon rind**
75 g (3 oz) **plain flour**
1 large **egg**, beaten
75 g (3 oz) **dried white breadcrumbs**
salt and **pepper**

To serve
new potatoes
broccoli florets

Cut deep slits along the sides of the chicken breasts to create a pocket in each. Mix together the cream cheese garlic, parsley and lemon juice and rind. Season well with salt and pepper, then spoon the filling into the chicken.

Place the flour, egg and breadcrumbs in separate shallow dishes. Coat each chicken breast first in the flour, then the egg and then the breadcrumbs and place on a baking sheet. Cook the chicken in a preheated oven, 220°C (425°F), Gas Mark 7, for 15–18 minutes until cooked through.

Serve the crisp baked chicken with steamed broccoli and boiled new potatoes.

For chicken fillets in garlic & herb breadcrumbs,
mix together 75 g (3 oz) dried white breadcrumbs with 1 teaspoon each of garlic powder and dried herbes de Provence in a shallow dish. Put 75 g (3 oz) plain flour in a separate dish and 1 beaten egg in another dish. Coat 500 g (1 lb) chicken mini-fillets in the flour, then the egg, then in breadcrumbs, and place on a baking sheet. Place in a preheated oven, 220°C (425°F), Gas Mark 7, for 12–15 minutes until cooked through, then serve with mashed potatoes and a mixed leaf salad. **Total cooking time 20 minutes.**

chicken koftas

Serves **4**

Total cooking time **20 minutes**

500 g (1 lb) **minced chicken**
2 **garlic cloves**, crushed
1 teaspoon **ground cumin**
2 teaspoons **ground coriander**
2 teaspoons chopped **fresh coriander**
200 g (7 oz) **Greek yogurt**
1 tablespoon **mint sauce**
¼ **cucumber**, coarsely grated and squeezed to remove excess liquid
salt and **pepper**

To serve
4 **pitta breads**, warmed and halved
salad leaves
baby plum tomatoes, halved

Put the minced chicken, garlic, cumin, ground coriander and fresh coriander in a bowl. Season with salt and pepper and mix well.

Using wet hands, make 12 even-sized sausage shapes from the mixture and thread on to metal skewers, pressing firmly. Cook under a preheated hot grill for 10 minutes, turning occasionally, until cooked through and browned.

Meanwhile, mix together the yogurt, mint sauce and cucumber. Take the koftas off the skewers and serve in warmed pitta breads with salad leaves, tomatoes and the yogurt dressing.

For quick chicken moussaka, fry 500 g (1 lb) minced chicken in 1 tablespoon sunflower oil until browned. Add 1 crushed garlic clove, 1 teaspoon ground cumin, 2 teaspoons ground coriander and a 400 g (13 oz) can chopped tomatoes. Simmer for 10 minutes. Meanwhile, thinly slice 1 aubergine, brush with a little oil and cook in a hot frying pan for 2 minutes on each side. Tip the mince mixture into a baking dish and arrange the aubergine slices on top. Cover with 200 g (7 oz) Greek yogurt mixed with 1 egg. Cook under a preheated medium grill until golden and bubbling. Serve with a green salad. **Total cooking time 30 minutes.**

hot & spicy

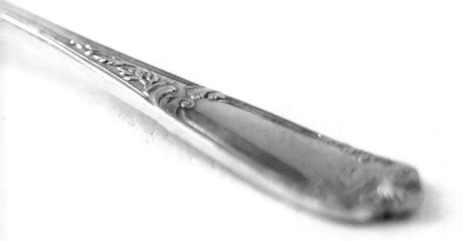

chicken noodle broth

Serves **4**
Total cooking time **30 minutes**

4 **skinless chicken thighs**,
about 350 g (11½ oz) total
weight
1.2 litres (2 pints) **chicken** or
vegetable stock
2 tablespoons **vegetable oil**
1 **red pepper**, cored,
deseeded and sliced
4 **spring onions**, cut into
1.5 cm (¾ inch) lengths
1 tablespoon peeled and
chopped **fresh root ginger**
200 g (7 oz) **button
mushrooms**, sliced
250 g (8 oz) **dried medium
egg noodles**
1–2 tablespoons **dark soy
sauce**
2 tablespoons chopped **fresh
coriander**

Place the chicken thighs in a saucepan and pour over
the stock. Bring to the boil, then reduce the heat and
simmer gently for about 20 minutes or until the chicken
is cooked through.

Meanwhile, heat the oil in a large saucepan or wok,
add the red pepper and spring onions and cook for
4–5 minutes. Add the ginger and mushrooms and
cook gently for a further 4–5 minutes until softened
and golden.

Use a slotted spoon to remove the chicken thighs
from the stock and set aside to cool slightly. Add the
noodles to the stock, turn off the heat, cover and set
aside for 4–5 minutes until just tender. Add the cooked
vegetables and season to taste with the soy sauce.

Once the chicken thighs are cool enough to handle,
remove and discard the bones, then shred the meat
and return to the soup. Ladle the soup and noodles into
4 large bowls. Scatter with the chopped coriander and
serve immediately.

For chicken noodle salad, cook 250 g (8 oz) medium
dried egg noodles according to the packet instructions.
Cool under cold running water. Meanwhile, slice 1
red pepper, 4 spring onions and 200 g (7 oz) button
mushrooms. Combine 4 tablespoons vegetable oil, 2
teaspoons sesame oil, 2 tablespoons light soy sauce
and 2 teaspoons minced ginger (from a jar). Toss the
noodles with 400 g (13 oz) shredded ready-cooked
chicken breasts, the vegetables and dressing, then serve
immediately, scattered with 2 tablespoons chopped fresh
coriander. **Total cooking time 10 minutes.**

chicken, chilli & rosemary soup

Serves **4**
Total cooking time **10 minutes**

2 x 400 g (13 oz) cans **cream
of chicken soup**
2 **garlic cloves**, crushed
1 **red chilli**, deseeded and
finely chopped, plus extra to
garnish
2 tablespoons finely chopped
rosemary
crusty bread rolls, to serve

To garnish
finely chopped **chives**
chilli oil

Pour the soup into a saucepan, stir in the garlic, chilli
and rosemary and bring to the boil. Reduce the heat to
medium and cook for a few minutes or until piping hot.

Remove from the heat. Ladle into bowls, sprinkle with
the chives and the remaining chopped chilli, to garnish,
and drizzle with chilli oil. Serve immediately with crusty
bread rolls.

For creamy chicken, chilli & rosemary pasta,
cook 350 g (11½ oz) penne in a large saucepan of
salted boiling water according to the packet instructions
until 'al dente'. Meanwhile, heat 2 tablespoons olive oil
in a large frying pan, add 2 chopped garlic cloves,
2 deseeded and finely chopped red chillies and
400 g (13 oz) chopped skinless chicken thigh fillets,
and cook over a medium heat, stirring occasionally, for
8–10 minutes or until the chicken is sealed and cooked
through. Add 1 teaspoon dried rosemary and 200 ml
(7 fl oz) crème fraîche. Drain the pasta, add to the frying
pan and season. Toss to mix well, then serve immediately
with a rocket salad. **Total cooking time 20 minutes.**

curried chicken & grape salad

Serves **4**
Total cooking time **10 minutes**

4 large **ready-cooked chicken
    breasts,** skin-on, cut into
    bite-sized pieces
large handful of **Baby Gem
    lettuce leaves**
200 g (7 oz) **cherry tomatoes,**
    halved
200 g (7 oz) **seedless green
    grapes,** halved
6 **spring onions,** thinly sliced

Curry mayonnaise
200 ml (7 fl oz) **mayonnaise**
2 teaspoons **medium** or **hot
    curry powder**
finely grated rind and juice of
    1 **lemon**
20 g (¾ oz) **fresh coriander,**
    finely chopped

Make the curry mayonnaise. Put all the ingredients
in a bowl and stir to mix well. Set aside.

Put the chicken, lettuce leaves, tomatoes, grapes
and spring onions in a large salad bowl and mix well.

Spoon over the mayonnaise, toss to mix well and
serve with crusty bread, if liked.

For grilled chicken with curry mayonnaise, make
the curry mayonnaise as above. Put 4 large boneless,
skinless chicken breasts, about 150 g (5 oz) each,
in a bowl. Mix 6 tablespoons olive oil, 1 teaspoon
dried red chilli flakes, 2 teaspoons paprika, 2 crushed
garlic cloves and the grated rind and juice of 1 lemon
in a bowl, then season. Pour the mixture over the
chicken and toss. Cook under a preheated hot grill
for 6–8 minutes on each side or until cooked through.
Cover and leave to rest for 2–3 minutes. Serve with
the curry mayonnaise and salad. **Total cooking time
30 minutes.**

114

chicken & apricot couscous

Serves **4**

Total cooking time **20 minutes**

200 g (7 oz) **couscous**

1 tablespoon **hot curry powder**

5 tablespoons **extra virgin olive oil**

700 ml (1 pint 3 fl oz) hot **chicken stock**

100 g (3½ oz) **cashew nuts**

finely grated rind and juice of 1 **lemon**

1 **red chilli**, deseeded and chopped

4 tablespoons chopped **mint**

4 tablespoons chopped **fresh coriander**

100 g (3½ oz) **ready-to-eat dried apricots**, finely chopped

100 g (3½ oz) **dried cranberries**

2 **ready-cooked chicken breasts**, skin removed and roughly shredded

juice of 1 **orange**

salt and **pepper**

chopped **flat leaf parsley**, to serve

Put the couscous, curry powder and oil in a large heatproof bowl. Stir in the stock, then cover with clingfilm and leave to stand for 8–10 minutes, or according to the packet instructions, until the stock is absorbed.

Meanwhile, heat a small nonstick frying pan until hot, add the cashew nuts and dry-fry, stirring frequently, for 3–4 minutes or until toasted. Remove from the pan and set aside.

Fork through the couscous to separate the grains, then stir in the cashews and all the remaining ingredients. Season, toss to mix well and serve scattered with chopped parsley.

For spicy chicken & fruit couscous salad, put 400 g (13 oz) shredded ready-cooked chicken breasts and 2 x 250 g (8 oz) tubs ready-cooked roasted vegetable couscous in a large bowl. Mix together 4 tablespoons olive oil, 1 deseeded and finely diced red chilli, 50 g (2 oz) chopped ready-to-eat dried apricots, 50 g (2 oz) dried cranberries, 1 teaspoon hot curry powder and the juice of 2 limes in a bowl and season. Pour over the salad, toss and serve. **Total cooking time 10 minutes.**

green chicken skewers

Serves **4**
Total cooking time **30 minutes**

800 g (1¾ lb) **skinless chicken thigh fillets**, cut into bite-sized pieces
30 g (1 oz) **fresh coriander**, chopped
30 g (1 oz) **mint**, chopped
1 teaspoon **coarse black pepper**
juice of 2 **lemons**
1 teaspoon **light muscovado sugar**
2 teaspoons peeled and finely grated **fresh root ginger**
2 **garlic cloves**, crushed
200 ml (7 fl oz) **natural yogurt**
lemon wedges, to serve

Dip
125 ml (4 fl oz) **rice** or **wine vinegar**
2 tablespoons **caster sugar**
1 **red chilli**, finely diced
½ **red onion**, finely diced
6 tablespoons finely diced **cucumber**

Put the chicken in a shallow non-reactive bowl. Put the herbs, pepper, lemon juice, sugar, ginger, garlic and yogurt in a food processor or blender and blend until smooth. Pour the mixture over the chicken and toss to coat evenly, then cover and leave to marinate for 10–15 minutes.

Meanwhile, make the dip. Heat the vinegar and sugar in a small saucepan until the sugar has dissolved, then increase the heat and boil for 3 minutes until slightly syrupy. Remove from the heat and stir in the red chilli and red onion. Leave to cool. When cool, stir in the cucumber and set aside.

Thread the chicken on to 12 metal skewers, then cook under a preheated medium-hot grill for 4–5 minutes on each side or until cooked through.

Transfer the skewers on to 4 serving plates and drizzle over a little of the dip. Serve with the remaining dip and lemon wedges to squeeze over.

For warm green chicken & rice salad, heat a large nonstick wok, add a 600 g (1 lb 5 oz) tub ready-cooked pilau rice and stir-fry over a high heat for 3–4 minutes until piping hot. Remove from the heat. Stir in 400 g (13 oz) diced ready-cooked chicken breasts, 1 deseeded and finely chopped red chilli and a large handful each of chopped mint and coriander. Transfer to a large bowl, squeeze over the juice of 1 lime, season and toss to mix well. **Total cooking time 10 minutes.**

Thai-style chicken patties

Serves **4**
Total cooking time **30 minutes**

400 g (13 oz) **minced chicken**
400 g (13 oz) **raw peeled tiger prawns**
4 cm (1½ inch) length of trimmed **lemon grass stalk**, finely chopped
50 g (2 oz) **fresh coriander**, chopped
5 tablespoons chopped **mint**
1 tablespoon peeled and grated **fresh root ginger**
2 large **garlic cloves**, crushed
1 **red chilli**, deseeded and finely chopped
1 tablespoon **medium curry powder**
200 g (7 oz) **dried rice noodles**
2 tablespoons **sunflower oil**, for brushing
salt and **pepper**

To serve
lime wedges
sweet chilli dipping sauce

Put the chicken, prawns, lemon grass, chopped herbs, ginger, garlic, red chilli and curry powder in a food processor or blender and blitz until fairly smooth. Using wet hands, divide the mixture into 12 portions and shape each portion into a patty. Transfer to a nonstick baking sheet, cover and chill for 8–10 minutes.

Meanwhile, cook the rice noodles according to the packet instructions, then drain and keep warm.

Brush the patties with oil and season. Cook under a preheated medium-hot grill for about 10 minutes, turning once or twice, or until browned and just cooked through.

Transfer the patties on to 4 serving plates and serve with the rice noodles, lime wedges and a sweet chilli dipping sauce.

For chicken, prawn & lemon grass stir-fry, heat 2 tablespoons sunflower oil in a large wok or frying pan until hot, add 500 g (1 lb) minced chicken, 1 tablespoon green curry paste and 1 tablespoon lemon grass paste and stir-fry over a high heat for 3–4 minutes or until sealed and browned. Stir in 300 g (10 oz) cooked peeled prawns, 1 tablespoon light soy sauce and 1 tablespoon fish sauce and heat for 3–4 minutes until piping hot. Serve with noodles. **Total cooking time 10 minutes.**

curried chicken samosas

200 g (7 oz) **potatoes**, peeled
 and finely chopped
100 g (3½ oz) **frozen mixed
 vegetables,** such as peas,
 sweetcorn and carrots
200 g (7 oz) **ready-cooked
 chicken**, chopped
1 tablespoon **medium curry
 paste**
1 tablespoon **mango chutney**,
 plus extra to serve
8 sheets of **filo pastry**, thawed
 if frozen, folded in half
1 tablespoon **sunflower oil**
1 tablespoon **poppy seeds**

Cook the potatoes in a saucepan of lightly salted boiling water for 5 minutes, adding the frozen vegetables towards the end so that they thaw.

Meanwhile, mix together the chicken, curry paste and mango chutney. Drain the vegetables, add to the chicken and mix well.

Place 2 tablespoons of the mixture in the corner of a folded sheet of filo pastry. Fold the end of the pastry over the filling to make a triangle, then continue folding along the pastry, keeping the triangular shape until the pastry is used up. Place on a baking sheet and repeat with remaining filling and pastry to make 8 samosas.

Brush the tops of the samosas with oil, sprinkle with poppy seeds and bake in a preheated oven, 200°C (400°F), Gas Mark 6, for 15 minutes until golden and crisp. Serve with mango chutney.

For curried chicken & rice, mix together 250 g (8 oz) ready-cooked basmati rice with 1 tablespoon medium curry paste and 1 tablespoon mango chutney. Add 200 g (7 oz) chopped ready-cooked chicken and 125 g (4 oz) frozen mixed vegetables. Heat in a microwave oven for 5 minutes until hot. Serve with extra mango chutney and poppadums. **Total cooking time 10 minutes.**

piquant chicken brochettes

Serves **4**
Total cooking time **20 minutes**

800 g (1¾ lb) **skinless chicken breast fillets**, cut into bite-sized pieces
finely grated rind and juice of **1 lemon**
1 red chilli, deseeded and finely chopped
1 teaspoon **hot smoked paprika**
100 ml (3½ fl oz) **extra virgin olive oil**
1 tablespoon **dried oregano**
3 **garlic cloves**, crushed
1 **onion**, cut into large pieces
1 **red pepper**, cored, deseeded and cut into large pieces
1 **yellow pepper**, cored, deseeded and cut into large pieces
salt and **pepper**

Put the chicken in a shallow non-reactive bowl. Mix together the lemon rind and juice, chilli, smoked paprika, oil, oregano and garlic in a bowl, then season well. Pour the mixture over the chicken and toss to coat evenly.

Thread the chicken on to 8 metal skewers, alternating with the onion and red and yellow peppers. Cook under a preheated medium-hot grill for 4–5 minutes on each side or until the chicken is cooked through.

Transfer the brochettes to 4 serving plates and serve with lemon wedges to squeeze over, if liked.

For piquant chicken & mixed pepper salad, put

4 roughly shredded ready-cooked chicken breasts, 400 g (13 oz) drained mixed roasted peppers from a jar and a handful of wild rocket leaves in a large salad bowl. Mix together 1 teaspoon chilli paste, 6 tablespoons extra virgin olive oil, 1 teaspoon clear honey and the juice of 1 large lemon in a bowl, then season. Pour the dressing over the salad, toss to mix well and serve. **Total cooking time 10 minutes.**

spicy chicken pancakes

Serves **4**
Total cooking time **20 minutes**

2 tablespoons **butter**, plus
  extra for greasing
300 g (10 oz) **baby chestnut
  mushrooms**, sliced
6 **spring onions**, finely sliced
2 **garlic cloves**, crushed
1 tablespoon **hot curry
  powder**
1 **red chilli**, deseeded and
  sliced
500 g (1 lb) pot **four cheese
  sauce**
300 g (10 oz) **baby spinach
  leaves**
2 **ready-cooked chicken
  breasts**, shredded
4 tablespoons chopped **fresh
  coriander**
8 **shop-bought savoury
  pancakes**, thawed if frozen
50 g (2 oz) **Parmesan
  cheese**, grated
salt and **pepper**
mixed salad, to serve

Heat the butter in a large frying pan, add the
mushrooms, spring onions, garlic, curry powder and red
chilli and cook over a high heat for 4–5 minutes, stirring
frequently, until the mushrooms are softened. Stir in
half of the cheese sauce and heat until just bubbling.
Add the spinach and cook for 1 minute or until just
wilted. Remove from the heat, stir in the chicken and
coriander and season.

Place 1 pancake on a clean work surface and spoon
one-eighth of the mushroom and spinach mixture
down the centre. Carefully roll the pancake up and
put into a shallow greased gratin dish. Repeat with
the remaining pancakes.

Drizzle the remaining cheese sauce over the pancakes,
sprinkle with the Parmesan and season to taste. Cook
under a preheated medium-hot grill for 3–4 minutes or
until piping hot and golden. Serve with a mixed salad.

**For chicken, mushroom & spinach salad with spicy
yogurt dressing**, put 4 shredded ready-cooked chicken
breasts, 200 g (7 oz) baby spinach leaves and 200 g
(7 oz) thinly sliced button mushrooms in a salad bowl.
Mix together 300 ml (½ pint) natural yogurt with
1 tablespoon mild curry powder, 2 tablespoons chopped
fresh coriander and the juice of 1 lemon in a bowl, then
season. Drizzle over the salad, toss to mix well and
serve. **Total cooking time 10 minutes.**

vietnamese herby chicken rice

Serves **4**
Total cooking time **30 minutes**

350 g (11½ oz) **long-grain
  rice**, rinsed and drained
850 ml (1 pint 9 fl oz) **chicken
  stock**
400 g (13 oz) **skinless
  chicken thigh fillets**, sliced
6 **shallots**, finely sliced
2 **red chillies**, finely sliced
2 teaspoons peeled and
  grated **fresh root ginger**
handful of **mint**, chopped
handful of **fresh coriander**,
  chopped
8 **spring onions**, finely sliced

Nuoc cham sauce
2 **garlic cloves**, chopped
1 **red chilli**, chopped
1 **lime**
3–4 tablespoons **fish sauce**
1–2 tablespoons **water**

Make the nuoc cham sauce. Put the garlic and red
chilli in a mortar and mash with the pestle to form a
paste. Squeeze the juice of the lime into the paste, then
remove the pulp and add it to the mixture. Mash to a
paste again, then stir in enough fish sauce and water
to dilute. Set aside.

Put the rice in a heavy-based saucepan, then stir in
the stock, chicken, shallots, red chillies and ginger and
bring to the boil. Cover tightly, reduce the heat to low
and cook, undisturbed, for 12–15 minutes or until the
liquid is absorbed, the rice is tender and the chicken is
cooked through.

Remove the pan from the heat and stir in the herbs
and spring onions. Cover and leave to stand for a few
minutes.

Ladle into warm bowls and serve with the nuoc cham
sauce spooned over or in a bowl on the side.

For Vietnamese chicken, herb & rice salad, put
500 g (1 lb) ready-cooked basmati rice, 400 g (13 oz)
shredded ready-cooked chicken breasts, 1 shredded
cucumber, 1 finely chopped red chilli and a small
handful each of chopped mint and coriander in a large
salad bowl. Make the nuoc cham sauce as above, then
spoon 2 tablespoons over the salad. Toss to mix well
and serve. **Total cooking time 10 minutes.**

spiced chicken stew

Serves **4**
Total cooking time **30 minutes**

2 tablespoons **olive oil**
800 g (1¾ lb) **skinless chicken breast fillets,** cut into bite-sized pieces
1 large **onion**, thinly sliced
4 **garlic cloves**, finely chopped
1 teaspoon peeled and finely grated **fresh root ginger**
1 **red chilli**, deseeded and finely chopped
2 teaspoons **ground cumin**
3 **cinnamon sticks**
¼ teaspoon **ground turmeric**
2 large **carrots**, peeled and cut into bite-sized pieces
large pinch of **saffron threads**
750 ml (1¼ pints) hot **chicken stock**
1 tablespoon **rose harissa paste**
8 **green olives**, pitted
8 **black olives**, pitted
6 small **preserved lemons**, halved
salt and **pepper**

Heat the oil in a large, heavy-based saucepan, add the chicken and onion and cook over a high heat for 2–3 minutes, stirring occasionally, until browned. Add the garlic, ginger, red chilli, cumin, cinnamon sticks and turmeric and fry, stirring, for 30 seconds.

Stir in the carrots, saffron and stock and bring to the boil. Reduce the heat to medium and cook, uncovered, for 15–20 minutes or until the chicken is cooked through and the carrots are tender.

Add the harissa, olives and preserved lemons, season to taste and stir to mix well. Ladle into warm bowls and serve immediately.

For spicy lemon chicken salad, put 4 roughly shredded ready-cooked chicken breasts and the leaves from 1 cos (Romaine) lettuce in a large serving dish. Mix together the juice of 1 lemon, 2 tablespoons finely chopped preserved lemons, 2 teaspoons harissa paste, 1 tablespoon clear honey and 6 tablespoons olive oil in a bowl. Season and serve with the salad. **Total cooking time 10 minutes.**

sweet & spicy chicken noodles

Serves **4**

Total cooking time **20 minutes**

300 g (10 oz) **dried medium egg noodles**

2 tablespoons **sunflower oil**

400 g (13 oz) **skinless chicken breast fillets**, cubed

300 g (10 oz) **ready-prepared stir-fry vegetables**

2 **red chillies**, deseeded and sliced

1 **garlic clove**, crushed

1 tablespoon **cornflour**

6 tablespoons **light soy sauce**

5 tablespoons **sweet chilli sauce**

1 tablespoon **rice wine vinegar**

4 tablespoons **passata**

1 tablespoon **soft light brown sugar**

½ teaspoon **ground ginger**

50 ml (2 fl oz) **water**

200 g (7 oz) **pineapple flesh**, cut into small pieces

4 **spring onions**, thinly sliced

Cook the noodles according to the packet instructions, then drain and keep warm.

Meanwhile, heat the oil in a large wok or frying pan until hot, add the chicken and stir-fry over a medium-high heat for 6–8 minutes or until lightly browned and just cooked through. Add the stir-fry vegetables and stir-fry for a further 3–4 minutes.

Mix together the red chillies, garlic, cornflour, soy sauce, chilli sauce, vinegar, passata, sugar and ground ginger in a small bowl. Add this mixture to the wok with the measurement water, pineapple and spring onions and stir-fry for 2–3 minutes or until all the ingredients are well coated.

Add the reserved noodles to the wok, toss to mix well and heat until piping hot. Divide into warm bowls and serve immediately.

For sweet & spicy chicken & pea rice, heat 2 tablespoons sunflower oil in a large wok until hot, add 500 g (1 lb) ready-cooked rice, 300 g (10 oz) frozen peas, 1 tablespoon sweet chilli sauce, 4 tablespoons light soy sauce, 1 tablespoon garlic paste and 1 tablespoon ginger paste and stir-fry over a high heat for 4–5 minutes. Add 400 g (13 oz) diced ready-cooked chicken breasts and stir-fry for 2–3 minutes or until piping hot. **Total cooking time 10 minutes.**

harissa chicken

Serves **4**

Total cooking time **30 minutes**

3 tablespoons **olive oil**

1 large **onion**, roughly chopped

450 g (14½ oz) **skinless chicken breast fillets**, sliced

½ teaspoon **ground cinnamon**

1 teaspoon **ground cumin**

1 teaspoon **ground coriander**

2 tablespoons **harissa**

400 g (13 oz) can **chopped tomatoes**

150 ml (¼ pint) hot **chicken stock**

400 g (13 oz) can **chickpeas**, rinsed and drained

couscous, to serve

Heat the oil in a large, heavy-based wok or frying pan, add the onion and chicken and cook over a high heat for 5 minutes. Add the spices and cook, stirring, for 2 minutes.

Add the harissa and continue to cook for a further 2 minutes before adding the chopped tomatoes and stock. Bring to the boil, reduce the heat, cover and gently simmer for 15 minutes, stirring occasionally.

Stir in the drained chickpeas and cook for a further 2 minutes until piping hot. Serve with couscous.

For yogurt & harissa chicken kebabs, cut 450 g (14½ oz) skinless chicken breast fillets into cubes and put them in a bowl with 4 tablespoons natural yogurt, 1 tablespoon harissa, a pinch each of cinnamon, cumin and coriander and 2 tablespoons chopped fresh coriander. Toss well to coat the chicken. Thread on to 4 metal skewers and place on a foil-lined grill rack with 175 g (6 oz) cherry tomatoes. Grill the kebabs and cherry tomatoes for 8–10 minutes, turning once, or until lightly charred and cooked through. Serve with couscous. **Total cooking time 20 minutes.**

curried chicken & peas

Serves **4**
Total cooking time **30 minutes**

3 tablespoons **vegetable oil**
2 teaspoons **cumin seeds**
2 **onions**, finely chopped
1 tablespoon peeled and
  grated **fresh root ginger**
1 tablespoon grated **garlic**
500 g (1 lb) **minced chicken**
2 tablespoons **ground
  coriander**
1 teaspoon **hot chilli powder**
1 tablespoon **ground cumin**
1 tablespoon **garam masala**
1 **red pepper**, cored,
  deseeded and finely
  chopped
100 g (3½ oz) **frozen peas**
2 **ripe tomatoes**, finely
  chopped
juice of ½ **lime**
chopped **fresh coriander
  leaves**, to garnish

To serve
warm **chapatis** or **parathas**
natural yogurt

Heat the oil in a large wok or frying pan until hot, add the cumin seeds and stir-fry over a medium heat for 1 minute. Add the onions and stir-fry for a further 3–4 minutes until softened, then add the ginger and garlic and continue to stir-fry for 1 minute.

Add the minced chicken and the ground spices and stir-fry for 5–7 minutes or until sealed and lightly browned. Stir in the red pepper, peas and tomatoes and stir-fry for a further 3–4 minutes or until cooked through and piping hot.

Remove from the heat and stir in the lime juice. Spoon into warm bowls, scatter with chopped coriander and serve with warm chapatis or parathas and a dollop of yogurt, sprinkled with a little garam masala.

For quick chicken & pea curry, heat 2 tablespoons olive oil in a large wok until hot, add 600 g (1 lb 5 oz) minced chicken and 2 tablespoons green curry paste and stir-fry over a high heat for 3–4 minutes or until the chicken is cooked through. Stir in a 400 ml (14 fl oz) can coconut milk and 100 g (3½ oz) frozen peas and cook for a further 3–4 minutes. Season well, then serve with jasmine rice or crusty bread. **Total cooking time 10 minutes.**

cold chicken with salsa verde

Serves **4**

Total cooking time **10 minutes**

1 x 1.5 kg (3 lb) **ready-cooked roast chicken**

Spicy salsa verde

2 tablespoons **red wine vinegar**

40 g (1 ½ oz) **flat leaf parsley**, chopped

20 g (¾ oz) **basil** or **mint**, chopped

2 **garlic cloves**, crushed

2 **red chillies**, deseeded and finely chopped

4 **anchovy fillets in oil**, drained and chopped

2 tablespoons **salted capers**, rinsed

125 ml (4 fl oz) **extra virgin olive oil**, plus extra if needed

pepper

Make the spicy salsa verde. Pour the vinegar into the bowl of a mini food processor, then add the herbs and pulse to form a coarse paste. Add the garlic, red chillies, anchovies and capers and whizz again to a coarse paste. Gradually add the oil through the feed tube with the motor still running, but do not over-process. Season with pepper.

Joint the chicken and transfer on to 4 plates. Spoon over the spicy salsa verde and serve.

For poached chicken with spicy salsa verde, put 4 large boneless, skinless chicken breasts in a large saucepan and pour over 800 ml (1 pint 8 fl oz) hot chicken stock. Add 1 bay leaf, 1 chopped carrot, 2 chopped celery sticks and 1 quartered onion. Bring to the boil, then reduce the heat to medium and cook, uncovered, for 20 minutes or until the chicken is cooked through. Meanwhile, make the salsa verde as above. Remove the chicken from the pan with a slotted spoon and drain on kitchen paper. Slice the chicken and serve with the salsa verde. **Total cooking time 30 minutes.**

chicken with chilli & rocket pesto

Serves **4**
Total cooking time **30 minutes**

600 g (1 lb 5 oz) **midi vine
  tomatoes**
olive oil, for brushing
4 large **boneless, skinless
  chicken breasts**
salt and **pepper**

Pesto
4 **garlic cloves**, crushed
2 **red chillies**, deseeded and
  finely chopped
30 g (1 oz) **basil**
40 g (1 oz) **rocket leaves**
50 g (2 oz) **Parmesan
  cheese**, grated
100 g (3½ oz) **pine nuts**,
  toasted
150 ml (¼ pint) **extra virgin
  olive oil**, plus extra if needed

Brush the tomatoes with olive oil and season well.
Place on a nonstick baking sheet and cook in a
preheated oven, 220°C (425°F), Gas Mark 7, for
10–12 minutes.

Meanwhile, lay a chicken breast between 2 sheets
of clingfilm and flatten slightly with a rolling pin or
meat mallet. Repeat with the remaining chicken
breasts. Brush lightly with oil and season. Heat a griddle
pan until smoking hot, add the chicken and cook for
5–6 minutes on each side or until cooked through.
Remove the chicken and leave to rest for 2–3 minutes.

While the chicken is cooking, make the pesto. Put all
the ingredients in a food processor or blender and blend
until fairly smooth, adding a little more oil for a runnier
consistency, if liked.

Transfer the chicken on to 4 warm serving plates,
drizzle over the pesto and serve with the roasted vine
tomatoes.

For chicken salad with chilli & rocket pesto, make
the pesto as above. Put 4 thinly sliced ready-cooked
chicken breasts and 400 g (13 oz) halved midi vine
tomatoes in a salad bowl. Drizzle over the pesto, toss to
mix well and serve. **Total cooking time 10 minutes.**

spicy vietnamese chicken

Serves **4**
Total cooking time **20 minutes**

3 tablespoons **sunflower oil**
800 g (1¾ lb) **skinless
chicken breast fillets**, cut
into strips
12 **spring onions**, cut into
3 cm (1 inch) lengths
4 **garlic cloves**, finely chopped
1 **red chilli**, deseeded and
finely sliced
2 **star anise**
8 cm (3 inch) length of
trimmed **lemon grass stalk**,
finely chopped
1 teaspoon crushed
cardamom seeds
1 **cinnamon stick**
300 g (10 oz) **mangetout**,
sliced
1 **carrot**, peeled and cut into
batons
2 tablespoons **fish sauce**
3 tablespoons **oyster sauce**

To garnish
handful of **fresh coriander,**
chopped
handful of **mint**, chopped
chopped **roasted peanuts**

Heat half the oil in a large wok or frying pan until
hot, add the chicken and stir-fry over a high heat for
3–4 minutes or until lightly browned and just cooked
through. Remove with a slotted spoon and keep warm.

Heat the remaining oil in the wok or pan until hot, add
the spring onions and stir-fry for 1–2 minutes until
softened. Add the garlic, red chilli, star anise, lemon
grass, cardamom, cinnamon stick, mangetout and
carrot and stir-fry for a further 3–4 minutes or until
the vegetables are softened.

Return the chicken to the wok or pan with the fish
sauce and oyster sauce and continue to stir-fry for
3–4 minutes or until the chicken is cooked through
and piping hot.

Spoon into warm bowls, scatter with chopped herbs
and peanuts and serve immediately.

For Vietnamese chicken soup, put 800 ml (1 pint
8 fl oz) chicken stock, 1 tablespoon lemon grass paste,
1 teaspoon chilli paste, 1 teaspoon garlic paste and
1 teaspoon ground cinnamon in a pan and bring to
the boil. Stir in 400 g (13 oz) shredded ready-cooked
chicken breasts and cook for 1–2 minutes or until
piping hot. **Total cooking time 10 minutes.**

thai red curry with chicken balls

Serves **4**

Total cooking time **30 minutes**

500 g (1 lb) **minced chicken**
1 tablespoon **lemon grass paste**
1 teaspoon **minced ginger paste**
7 tablespoons chopped **fresh coriander**
1 small **red bird's eye chilli**, finely chopped
1 tablespoon **vegetable oil**
2 tablespoons **red Thai curry paste**
400 ml (14 fl oz) can **coconut milk**
salt and **pepper**

Put the mince in a large bowl with the lemon grass paste, ginger paste, 3 tablespoons of the chopped fresh coriander and the chopped red chilli. Season well with a little salt and pepper and mix well with a fork to blend the spices into the chicken. Shape the mixture into 32 walnut-sized balls.

Heat the oil in a large, heavy-based frying pan and cook the meatballs over a high heat for 8–10 minutes, in batches if necessary, until golden in places, lightly shaking the pan to turn the meatballs. Mix the curry paste into the coconut milk and pour over the meatballs. Bring to the boil, then reduce the heat and simmer for 5 minutes until the chicken balls are cooked through. Stir in the remaining fresh coriander and serve with boiled rice, if liked.

For Thai chicken burgers, put 375 g (12 oz) minced chicken in a bowl with 1 tablespoon Thai curry paste and 3 tablespoons chopped fresh coriander. Shape the flavoured mince into 4 patty shapes and flatten as much as possible without the patties breaking. Heat 1 tablespoon vegetable oil in a large, heavy-based frying pan and cook the patties for 2–3 minutes on each side over a high heat until golden and cooked through. Serve in buns with salad. **Total cooking time 10 minutes.**

chicken biryani

Serves **4**
Total cooking time **30 minutes**

250 g (8 oz) **easy-cook basmati rice**
2 tablespoons **vegetable oil**
1 **large onion**, thinly sliced
300 g (10 oz) **skinless chicken breast fillets**, diced
1 **bay leaf**
3 **cardamom pods**
1 teaspoon ground **turmeric**
4 tablespoons **curry paste**
150 ml (¼ pint) **chicken stock**
75 g (3 oz) **raisins**
4 tablespoons **natural yogurt**
50 g (2 oz) **toasted flaked almonds**
4 tablespoons chopped **fresh coriander**, to garnish

Cook the rice in a large saucepan of lightly salted boiling water for 15–20 minutes or until tender.

Meanwhile, heat the oil in a large, heavy-based frying pan, add the onion and chicken and cook over a medium-high heat for 5–8 minutes or until golden, adding the bay leaf, cardamom and turmeric for the final 1 minute of cooking.

Add the curry paste and stir-fry for 1 minute, then pour in the stock. Bring to the boil, add the raisins and yogurt and cook gently for 10 minutes until the stock has reduced by half.

Drain the cooked rice, add to the pan with the chicken and toss and cook for 2–3 minutes. Scatter with flaked almonds and garnish with chopped fresh coriander.

For simple fruity chicken biryani, cook 250 g (8 oz) express rice and set aside. Heat 1 tablespoon vegetable oil in a heavy-based frying pan and cook 250 g (8 oz) diced skinless chicken breast fillets over a high heat for 8 minutes or until golden and cooked through. Add 2 tablespoons curry paste, 75 g (3 oz) raisins and 4 tablespoons flaked almonds and toss well in the pan. Add the cooked rice and toss again before garnishing with fresh coriander to serve. **Total cooking time 10 minutes.**

spicy chicken risotto

Serves **4**

Total cooking time **30 minutes**

50 g (2 oz) **unsalted butter**
1 tablespoon **olive oil**
1 **onion**, finely chopped
1 **red chilli**, deseeded and
  finely chopped
2 **garlic cloves**, finely chopped
1 **celery stick**, finely chopped
1 **carrot**, peeled and finely
  chopped
275 g (9 oz) **risotto rice**
100 ml (3½ fl oz) **dry white
  wine**
3 **ready-cooked chicken
  breasts**, diced
900 ml (1 ½ pints) hot
  vegetable stock
100 g (3½ oz) **Parmesan
  cheese,** finely grated
finely grated rind of 1 **lemon**
6 tablespoons finely chopped
  tarragon
salt and **pepper**

Heat the butter and oil in a large frying pan, add the onion, chilli, garlic, celery and carrot and cook over a medium heat for 3–4 minutes until softened. Add the rice and stir for 1 minute or until the grains are well coated. Pour in the wine and stir until it has been absorbed, then stir in the chicken.

Add 1 ladle of hot stock and simmer, stirring until it has been absorbed. Repeat with another ladle of stock, then reserve 1 ladle and continue to add the stock at intervals and cook as before, for a further 18–20 minutes or until the liquid has been absorbed and the rice is tender but still firm ('al dente').

Stir in the reserved stock, Parmesan, lemon rind and tarragon, season and mix well. Remove from the heat, cover and leave to stand for 2 minutes.

Spoon into warm bowls, season and serve immediately.

For chicken, lemon & tarragon baguettes, slice
2 warm medium baguettes into half horizontally and spread each with 2 tablespoons ready-made tarragon mayonnaise. Divide 2 sliced ready-cooked chicken breasts between the baguette bases, then sprinkle over the finely grated rind of ½ lemon and season. Top with the baguette lids, then cut each into 2 and serve. **Total cooking time 10 minutes.**

chicken & mango noodles

Total cooking time **10 minutes**

2 tablespoons **vegetable oil**
2 tablespoons **hot chilli sauce**
4 tablespoons **sweet chilli
    sauce**
4 tablespoons **dark soy sauce**
2 large **skinless chicken
    breast fillets**, cut into thin
    strips
200 g (7 oz) **fresh mango
    chunks**
300 g (10 oz) **ready-prepared
    stir-fry vegetables**
2 x 300 g (10 oz) **packs
    ready-cooked medium egg
    noodles**
75 g (3 oz) **dry-roasted
    peanuts**, chopped
salt and **pepper**

Mix together the oil, hot chilli sauce, sweet chilli sauce and soy sauce in a large bowl. Add the chicken strips, season and mix together.

Heat a large nonstick wok or frying pan until hot, then add the chicken, reserving the marinade, and stir-fry over a high heat for 5 minutes or until lightly browned and cooked through. Add the mango, stir-fry vegetables, noodles and the reserved marinade and stir-fry for a further few minutes until piping hot.

Mix in the chopped peanuts, then divide between 4 warm bowls. Serve immediately.

For spicy chicken & mango skewers, cut 4 large skinless chicken breast fillets into bite-sized pieces and place in a bowl with 1 tablespoon hot chilli sauce, 2 tablespoons sweet chilli sauce and 2 tablespoons light soy sauce. Stir to mix well. Thread the chicken on to 12 metal skewers, alternating with 400 g (13 oz) shop-bought fresh mango chunks. Cook under a preheated medium-hot grill for 4–5 minutes on each side or until the chicken is cooked through. Serve with a mixed leaf salad. **Total cooking time 20 minutes.**

thai green coconut chicken

Serves **4**
Total cooking time **30 minutes**

4 large **boneless chicken breasts**, skin on
1 teaspoon **Thai green curry paste**
4 tablespoons **coconut cream**
2 tablespoons **fresh white breadcrumbs**
finely grated rind of 1 **lime**
1 teaspoon **lemon grass paste**
sunflower oil, for drizzling
salt and **pepper**

To serve
steamed **jasmine rice**
steamed **Chinese greens**

Using a small, sharp knife, cut a slit down the side of each chicken breast to form a deep pocket. Mix together the remaining ingredients in a bowl, then season well. Divide the mixture evenly between the 4 chicken pockets.

Drizzle with a little oil, then transfer to a nonstick baking sheet. Place in a preheated oven, 180°C (350°F), Gas Mark 4, for 18–20 minutes or until the chicken is cooked through.

Serve with steamed jasmine rice and Chinese greens.

For quick Thai green chicken curry, heat 2 tablespoons sunflower oil in a large wok or frying pan until hot, add 2 tablespoons Thai green curry paste and stir-fry over a medium heat for 1–2 minutes. Stir in 4 diced ready-cooked chicken breasts and a 400 ml (14 fl oz) can coconut milk and bring to the boil. Cook for 3–4 minutes or until piping hot, then remove from the heat, season and stir in 4 tablespoons each of chopped fresh coriander and Thai basil leaves. Serve with steamed rice or noodles. **Total cooking time 10 minutes.**

family
favourites

honey & mustard chicken salad

Serves **4**
Total cooking time **20 minutes**

3 tablespoons **extra virgin olive oil**
1 teaspoon **clear honey**
1 teaspoon **Dijon mustard**
1 teaspoon **lemon juice**
3 **skinless, boneless chicken breasts**
2 tablespoons **pumpkin seeds**
75 g (3 oz) **watercress**
25 g (1 oz) **rocket leaves**
200 g (7 oz) **frozen peas**, thawed
1 large **avocado**, stoned, peeled, stoned and cut into slices

Whisk together the olive oil, honey, mustard and lemon juice in a small bowl to make a dressing.

Place the chicken breasts on a foil-lined baking sheet. Cook under a preheated hot grill for 5–6 minutes on each side or until cooked through.

Meanwhile, heat a small nonstick frying pan over a medium heat, add the pumpkin seeds and dry-fry until golden, stirring frequently. Remove from the pan and set aside.

Toss together the watercress and rocket and divide between 4 plates.

Slice the chicken diagonally and divide between the plates of salad leaves. Scatter over the peas, avocado and pumpkin seeds, pour over the dressing and serve immediately.

For chicken, avocado, watercress & mustard sandwiches, spread 4 slices of bread with 1 teaspoon wholegrain mustard. Divide 25 g (1 oz) watercress between the slices of bread, then top with 2 sliced honey-roasted chicken breasts and 1 large stoned, peeled and sliced avocado. Top with 4 more slices of bread to make 4 sandwiches. **Total cooking time 10 minutes.**

mexican chicken burgers

Serves **2**

Total cooking time **20 minutes**

2 **boneless, skinless chicken breasts**, about 150 g (5 oz) each, halved horizontally

2 teaspoons **fajita seasoning**

1 tablespoon **olive oil**

1 **red pepper**, cored, quartered and deseeded

2 tablespoons **soured cream** chopped **chives**

2 **soft burger buns**, halved

½ **avocado**, stoned, peeled and sliced

Tomato salad

5 **cherry tomatoes**, halved

½ small **red onion**, thinly sliced

½ **red chilli**, deseeded and chopped

1 tablespoon chopped **flat leaf parsley**

squeeze of **lime juice**

salt and **pepper**

Coat the chicken pieces in fajita seasoning, place on a foil-lined grill rack and drizzle with the oil, then add the pepper quarters, skin side up, to the grill rack. Cook under a preheated medium grill for 10–15 minutes, turning occasionally, until the chicken is cooked through and the peppers are soft and lightly charred.

Meanwhile, make the salad. Mix together all the ingredients in a bowl and season.

Mix together the soured cream and chives in a small bowl.

Toast the buns, then fill with avocado slices, the chicken and the grilled peppers. Top with spoonfuls of tomato salad and soured cream. Serve with the remaining tomato salad.

For fully loaded chicken nachos, spread out 200 g (7 oz) tortilla chips in an ovenproof dish. Scatter over 150 g (5 oz) chopped ready-cooked barbecue chicken. Top with 2 tablespoons tomato salsa. Add 1 tablespoon sliced jalapeño peppers from a jar and sprinkle with 75 g (3 oz) grated Cheddar cheese. Cook under a preheated hot grill for 3–4 minutes until melted and warm. Serve with ready-made guacamole. **Total cooking time 10 minutes.**

baked chicken with lime

Serves **4**
Total cooking time **30 minutes**

2 **limes**
2.5 cm (1 inch) piece of **fresh root ginger**, peeled and finely grated
1 teaspoon **Thai fish sauce**
1 tablespoon **groundnut** or **vegetable oil**
large bunch of **fresh coriander**
4 **boneless, skinless chicken breasts**, about 150 g (5 oz) each
350 g (11½ oz) **Thai rice**, rinsed
600 ml (1 pint) cold **water**
salt

Finely grate the rind from the 2 limes, squeeze the juice from one of them and finely slice the other.

Place the lime rind and juice in a mini-chopper with the ginger, fish sauce, oil and coriander, including the stalks. Blend to make a paste.

Cut 3 deep slashes diagonally into the chicken breasts and massage the paste all over the chicken. Place a slice of lime into each slash.

Place the chicken breasts in a roasting tin, cover with foil and bake in a preheated oven, 200°C (400°F), Gas Mark 6, for 18–20 minutes or until the chicken is cooked through.

Meanwhile, place the rice in a large saucepan with the measurement water, season with salt and bring to the boil. Reduce the heat, cover with a tight-fitting lid and cook very gently for 15–18 minutes until all of the water has been absorbed and the rice is tender and sticky. Serve the chicken with the sticky rice, drizzled with chicken juices.

For chicken & lime noodle salad, place 375 g (12 oz) cooked and cooled rice noodles in a serving bowl with 300 g (10 oz) ready-cooked chicken strips, the grated rind of 1 lime, a bunch of coriander, chopped, and 1 thinly sliced red pepper, then toss to combine. Pour 3 tablespoons vegetable oil into a small bowl with 2 tablespoons lime juice, 2 teaspoons grated fresh root ginger and 1 tablespoon fish sauce and whisk to combine. Drizzle the salad with the dressing to serve. **Total cooking time 10 minutes.**

chicken chilli pasta

Serves **4**
Total cooking time **20 minutes**

1 tablespoon **sunflower oil**
500 g (1 lb) **minced chicken**
1 **garlic clove**, crushed
1 teaspoon **chilli powder**
½ teaspoon **chilli flakes**
450 ml (¾ pint) **passata**
1 tablespoon **sun-dried
  tomato pesto**
375 g (12 oz) **spaghetti**
salt and **pepper**
freshly grated **Parmesan
  cheese**, to serve

Heat the oil in a large frying pan, add the minced chicken and fry over a high heat for 5 minutes, breaking up any clumps.

Add the garlic, chilli powder, chilli flakes, passata and pesto. Season with salt and pepper, bring to the boil, then reduce the heat and simmer for 10 minutes.

Meanwhile, cook the spaghetti in a saucepan of lightly salted boiling water for 8–10 minutes, or according to the packet instructions, until 'al dente'. Drain and toss with the chicken chilli sauce. Serve with plenty of freshly grated Parmesan cheese.

For baked chilli chicken, cut several slashes across the top of 4 boneless chicken breasts (with skin on). Place in a foil-lined baking tin and pour over a mixture of 5 tablespoons balsamic vinegar, 2 tablespoons lemon juice, 4 tablespoons olive oil and 1 chopped red chilli. Bake in a preheated oven, 200°C (400°F), Gas Mark 6, for 25 minutes with 500 g (1 lb) frozen roast potatoes in a separate baking tin until the chicken is cooked through and the potatoes are crisp. Serve with peas. **Total cooking time 30 minutes.**

chicken & tarragon burgers

Serves **4**
Total cooking time **20 minutes**

500 g (1 lb) **skinless chicken breast fillets**, roughly chopped
1 tablespoon **wholegrain mustard**
3 tablespoons chopped **tarragon**
½ small **red chilli**, finely chopped (optional)
4 **wholemeal buns**
pepper

To serve
béarnaise sauce from a jar
rocket leaves tossed in **lemon juice**

Place the chicken in a food processor and whizz until smooth. Transfer to a bowl, add the mustard, tarragon and chilli, if using, and season well with pepper. Mix together until well blended, then shape into 4 patties.

Lay the chicken burgers on a foil-lined grill rack and cook under a preheated hot grill for 4–5 minutes on each side until browned and cooked through. Split the buns and place, cut side up, under the grill for the final 1 minute of cooking time.

Place a hot burger on the top of each warm bun base and top with a spoonful of béarnaise sauce and a handful of lemon juice-dressed rocket. Cover with the warm bun tops and serve immediately.

For crunchy chicken burgers with tarragon mayonnaise, place 4 boneless, skinless chicken breasts, about 150 g (5 oz) each, between 2 sheets of lightly oiled clingfilm and bash with a rolling pin until half their original thickness. Beat 1 egg with 1 teaspoon Dijon mustard. Place 100 g (3½ oz) fresh white breadcrumbs in a separate bowl. Dip each chicken breast into the egg mixture and then coat in breadcrumbs. Cook under a preheated grill for 4 minutes on each side until crisp and brown. Meanwhile, stir 1 tablespoon chopped tarragon and 1 teaspoon lemon juice into 4 tablespoons mayonnaise. Serve on the burgers in toasted buns, with salad leaves. **Total cooking time 10 minutes.**

chicken & vegetable satay

Serves **4**

Total cooking time **20 minutes**

125 ml (4 fl oz) **tamari soy sauce**

3 tablespoons **smooth peanut butter**

1 tablespoons **water**

2 **skinless chicken breast fillets**, cut into strips

4 large **mushrooms**, halved

1 **red pepper**, cored, deseeded and cut into chunks

1 **yellow pepper**, cored, deseeded and cut into chunks

1 **courgette**, halved and sliced

½ **Chinese lettuce**, shredded

2 **carrots**, peeled and grated

25 g (1 oz) **bean sprouts**

small handful of **fresh coriander leaves**

2 teaspoons **sesame oil**

juice of **1 lime**

2 tablespoons **sesame seeds**, toasted, to serve

Mix together the tamari, peanut butter and measurement water in a large bowl.

Toss the chicken, mushrooms, peppers and courgette in the peanut mixture and thread on to 8 satay sticks that have been soaked in water to prevent burning.

Cook under a preheated hot grill for 12–14 minutes, turning frequently, until the chicken is cooked through.

Meanwhile, toss together the lettuce, grated carrots, bean sprouts and coriander leaves with the sesame oil and lime juice.

Serve the satay with the salad, sprinkled with toasted sesame seeds.

For chicken satay with satay sauce, stir-fry 225 g (7½ oz) peanuts in 100 ml (3½ fl oz) vegetable oil for 1 minute, then blitz until smooth. Fry 2 chopped garlic cloves and 4 chopped shallots for 30 seconds, then add 1 tablespoon tamari soy sauce, 1 teaspoon brown sugar, 1 diced red chilli, 400 ml (14 fl oz) water and the blended peanuts and simmer for 7–8 minutes to thicken. Meanwhile, grill 8 ready-made chicken satay sticks for 3–4 minutes on each side until cooked through. Stir the juice of 1 lemon into the satay sauce and serve with the chicken. **Total cooking time 10 minutes.**

166

soy chicken & rice noodles

Serves **2**
Total cooking time **10 minutes**

300 g (10 oz) **ready-cooked rice noodles**

2 tablespoons **soy sauce**

1 tablespoon **sesame** or **vegetable oil**

½ **red chilli**, deseeded and finely sliced or chopped (optional)

1 teaspoon peeled and grated **fresh root ginger**

150 g (5 oz) **ready-cooked chicken breast**, sliced or torn

2 **spring onions**, sliced

1 **red pepper** or 125 g (4 oz) **mangetout**, thinly sliced

Place the noodles in a sieve or colander and pour boiling water over them. Drain, then cool under cold running water. Drain well and place in a large bowl.

Whisk together the soy sauce, oil, chilli, if using, and ginger and drizzle the mixture over the noodles. Toss really well to coat, then add the remaining ingredients and mix gently to combine. Heap into bowls to serve.

For soy noodles with chicken, heat 2 tablespoons vegetable oil in a frying pan and cook 1 large, thinly sliced skinless chicken breast fillet over a medium-high heat for 5–6 minutes until lightly golden and just cooked through. Add 125 g (4 oz) sliced mangetout, 2 sliced spring onions, a 1.5 cm (¾ inch) piece of fresh root ginger, peeled and chopped, 2 sliced garlic cloves and ½ chopped red chilli. Stir-fry for 2–3 minutes until softened, then add 300 g (10 oz) straight-to-wok noodles and stir-fry for 3 minutes until piping hot. Pour in 2 tablespoons light soy sauce and 2 tablespoons oyster sauce, toss to coat and heap into bowls. **Total cooking time 20 minutes.**

lemon & parsley chicken skewers

Serves **2**
Total cooking time **15 minutes**

300 g (10 oz) **skinless
  chicken breast fillets,** cut
  into chunks
finely grated rind and juice of
  1 lemon
2 tablespoons **olive oil**
3 tablespoons finely chopped
  parsley
salt and **pepper**

To serve
rocket and tomato salad
warm **pitta breads**
200 g (7 oz) **ready-made
  tzatziki**

Place the chicken in a non-reactive bowl with the
lemon rind and juice and the oil and toss well to coat.
Stir in the parsley and season well.

Thread the chicken on to 4 small metal skewers and
cook under a preheated hot grill for 8–10 minutes until
golden and cooked through, turning once. Serve with a
simple rocket and tomato salad, warm pitta breads and
spoonfuls of tzatziki.

For lemon & parsley-stuffed chicken, make a slit
lengthways in the side of 2 boneless, skinless chicken
breasts, about 150 g (5 oz) each, to form pockets. Thinly
slice ½ lemon, then stuff the chicken with the lemon
slices. Press a small bunch of parsley into the cavities
and season. Tie around each piece once with a piece of
kitchen string. Heat 15 g (1 oz) butter and 1 tablespoon
olive oil in a frying pan, add the chicken and cook over
a medium-high heat for 7–8 minutes on each side until
golden and cooked through. Serve with tzatziki and a
simple salad. **Total cooking time 20 minutes.**

chicken pad thai

Serves **4**
Total cooking time **10 minutes**

3 tablespoons **vegetable oil**
1 **egg**, lightly beaten
1 **garlic clove**, crushed
2 teaspoons peeled and finely
grated **fresh root ginger**
2 **spring onions**, sliced
300 g (10 oz) **ready-cooked
rice noodles**
50 g (2 oz) **bean sprouts**
2 **ready-cooked chicken
breasts**, torn into thin strips
2 tablespoons **Thai fish sauce**
2 teaspoons **tamarind paste**
2 teaspoons **sugar**
pinch of **chilli powder**
25 g (1 oz) **ready-roasted
peanuts**, roughly chopped
handful of **fresh coriander**,
chopped

Heat a large wok until smoking hot. Add 1 tablespoon
of the oil and swirl around the pan, then pour in the egg.
Stir around the pan and cook for 1–2 minutes until just
cooked through. Remove from the wok and set aside.

Heat the remaining oil in the wok, add the garlic,
ginger and spring onions and cook for 2 minutes until
softened. Add the noodles to the pan along with the
bean sprouts and chicken.

Stir in the fish sauce, tamarind paste, sugar and chilli
powder and continue to cook, adding a splash of boiling
water if necessary. Heat through, then return the egg to
the pan and mix in. Divide between serving bowls and
scatter with the peanuts and coriander to serve.

For chicken noodle soup, simmer 1.2 litres
(2 pints) chicken stock with 3 tablespoons rice wine,
2 tablespoons light soy sauce and 1 star anise for
10 minutes. Mix 300 g (10 oz) minced chicken with
1 teaspoon peeled and grated fresh root ginger and
1 teaspoon soy sauce. Shape into balls and cook in
the soup for 7 minutes. Add 100 g (3½ oz) shiitake
mushrooms and cook for a further 3 minutes. Stir in
2 bok choi, quartered, and cook for 1 minute. Add
200 g (7 oz) ready-cooked rice noodles, heat through
and serve. **Total cooking time 30 minutes.**

chicken breasts with herb butter

Serves **4**
Total cooking time **20 minutes**

50 g (2 oz) **butter**, softened
grated rind of **1 lemon**
1 **garlic clove**, crushed
handful of **basil**, finely
  chopped
4 **boneless, skinless chicken
  breasts**
6 tablespoons **olive oil**, plus
  extra for greasing
100 g (3½ oz) **dried
  breadcrumbs**
25 g (1 oz) **Parmesan
  cheese**, grated
salt and **pepper**

Mix together the butter, lemon rind, garlic and basil and season to taste. Use a sharp knife to make a small horizontal slit in the side of each chicken breast to form a little pocket, making sure you don't cut all the way through the meat. Tuck some of the butter inside each breast, then smooth over to seal.

Rub 1 tablespoon of the oil over each chicken breast and season well. Put the breadcrumbs on a plate and dip each breast in the crumbs until well coated.

Transfer the chicken to a lightly greased baking tin, sprinkle over the Parmesan, drizzle with the remaining oil and cook in a preheated oven, 200°C (400°F), Gas Mark 6, for 20 minutes or until golden and cooked through. Serve with new potatoes and green beans.

For herby chicken sandwiches, mix together 6 tablespoons mayonnaise, the finely grated rind of ½ lemon and a handful of chopped basil. Cut 4 skinless chicken breast fillets into slices, season and rub with 2 tablespoons oil. Cook on a preheated griddle pan for 5 minutes, turning once, until seared and cooked through. Spread the mayonnaise on the cut sides of 4 split ciabatta rolls and fill with the warm chicken and some salad leaves. **Total cooking time 10 minutes.**

creamy cider chicken

Serves **4**

Total cooking time **30 minutes**

3 tablespoons **olive or vegetable oil**

8 **boneless chicken thighs**, about 625 g (1¼ lb) total weight, skin on

2–3 tablespoons seasoned **flour**

100 g (3½ oz) **back bacon**, chopped

100 g (3½ oz) **mushrooms**, sliced

200 ml (7 fl oz) boiling **vegetable** or **chicken stock**

250 ml (8 fl oz) **dry cider**

2 tablespoons **cider vinegar**

4 tablespoons **single cream** or **crème fraîche**

salt and **pepper**

Heat 2 tablespoons of the oil in a large, deep-sided frying pan. Dust the chicken with the seasoned flour and cook in the pan, skin side down, for about 10 minutes, until really golden and crisp.

Meanwhile, heat the remaining oil in a small frying pan and cook the bacon for 3–4 minutes until golden. Add the mushrooms and cook for a further 2–3 minutes until softened.

Turn the chicken thighs over, then add the bacon and mushrooms to the pan. Pour over the stock, cider and cider vinegar, bring to the boil, then reduce the heat and simmer gently for about 15 minutes until the chicken is cooked through.

Arrange the chicken thighs alongside the rice, then stir the cream into the pan. Season to taste with salt and pepper, then spoon the sauce over the chicken and serve with boiled rice.

For creamy chicken rice, heat 2 tablespoons vegetable oil in a frying pan and cook 100 g (3½ oz) chopped back bacon for 3–4 minutes until golden. Add 100 g (3½ oz) sliced mushrooms and cook for a further 2–3 minutes. Add 300 g (10 oz) diced ready-cooked chicken, 500 g (1 lb) cooked rice and 300 ml (½ pint) crème fraîche, then season well and stir over the heat for 1–2 minutes until hot. Spoon the creamy rice into 4 bowls to serve. **Total cooking time 10 minutes.**

sweet balsamic chicken

Serves **4**
Total cooking time **20 minutes**

6 tablespoons **balsamic vinegar**
4 **boneless, skinless chicken breasts**, about 150 g (5 oz) each
2 tablespoons **olive oil**
1 **onion**, thinly sliced
1 **red onion**, thinly sliced
2 tablespoons **clear honey**
1 tablespoon chopped **rosemary**
150 ml (¼ pint) **chicken stock**
pepper

To serve
mashed potatoes
green beans

Put the balsamic vinegar in a non-reactive bowl and season with pepper. Make 3 small cuts in the top of each of the chicken breasts. Add the chicken to the vinegar and toss to coat. Set aside for 3–4 minutes.

Meanwhile, heat the oil in a large, heavy-based frying pan and cook the onions over a medium-high heat for 5 minutes or until soft and beginning to turn golden. Add the chicken, cut side down, and cook for 3 minutes. Turn the chicken over and cook for a further 3 minutes.

Turn once more and add the balsamic vinegar from the bowl together with the honey and rosemary. Reduce the heat, add the stock, cover and simmer, stirring once, for 3–4 minutes or until the chicken is cooked through. Serve the chicken on warmed serving plates with the onions spooned over. Serve with mashed potatoes and green beans.

For balsamic chicken bruschetta, thinly slice 250 g (8 oz) skinless chicken breast fillets, each about 125 g (4 oz), and put in a non-reactive bowl with 3 tablespoons balsamic vinegar, 1 tablespoon clear honey and ½ teaspoon dried rosemary. Toss together. Heat 1 tablespoon olive oil in a large frying pan and cook the chicken over a high heat for 7–8 minutes until golden and cooked through. Meanwhile, slice 8 large mushrooms and add to the pan for the final 4 minutes of cooking. Lightly toast 4 diagonal slices of ciabatta, spoon the balsamic chicken and mushroom over the top of each slice and serve warm. **Total cooking time 10 minutes.**

mango & peanut chicken salad

Serves **4**
Total cooking time **10 minutes**

2 tablespoons **sesame oil**
350 g (11½ oz) **skinless chicken breast fillets,** thinly sliced
150 g (5 oz) **spinach and watercress salad**
1 large ripe **mango**, stoned, peeled and sliced
4 tablespoons **crunchy peanut butter**
5 tablespoons **coconut milk**
2 tablespoons **sweet chilli sauce**
4 tablespoons **water**

Heat 1 tablespoon of the sesame oil in a large, heavy-based frying pan, add the sliced chicken and cook over a high heat for 5–6 minutes, stirring frequently, until browned and cooked through.

Meanwhile, place the spinach and watercress salad with the mango in a large serving bowl, drizzle with the remaining sesame oil and toss to mix.

Add the remaining ingredients to the chicken in the frying pan and cook, stirring, for 1 minute. Toss into the salad and serve while still warm.

For chicken & mango kebabs, cut 3 skinless chicken breast fillets, about 175 g (6 oz) each, into cubes and place in a bowl with 4 tablespoons dark soy sauce, a 1 cm (½ inch) piece of fresh root ginger, peeled and chopped, and ½ teaspoon Chinese 5-spice powder. Toss well to coat, cover and leave to marinate for 5 minutes. Meanwhile, stone, peel and cut 1 mango into large chunks. Toss in a bowl with 1 tablespoon sesame oil and 2 tablespoons chopped fresh coriander. Thread the chicken and mango evenly on to 8 metal skewers. Cook the kebabs under a preheated hot grill for 8–10 minutes, turning occasionally, until browned and cooked through. **Total cooking time 20 minutes.**

chicken & tarragon pesto penne

Serves **4**
Total cooking time **10 minutes**

300 g (10 oz) **penne**
125 ml (4 fl oz) **olive oil**
75 g (3 oz) **Parmesan
  cheese**, grated
handful of **tarragon leaves**
75 g (3 oz) **pine nuts**, toasted
1 **garlic clove**, crushed
grated rind and juice of 1
  lemon
3 **ready-cooked chicken
  breasts**, sliced
100 g (3½ oz) **watercress**
12 **baby tomatoes**, quartered

Cook the penne in a large saucepan of boiling water
for 8–9 minutes, or according to the packet instructions
until 'al dente'. Drain and refresh under cold running
water, then toss with 2 tablespoons of the oil.

Meanwhile, place the Parmesan, tarragon, pine nuts,
garlic and lemon rind in a food processor and process
for 1 minute. Then, while the motor is still running,
gradually pour in the remaining olive oil through the
feed tube to form the pesto.

Toss the pesto with the pasta, chicken, watercress,
tomatoes and lemon juice, and serve.

For chicken & tarragon tagliatelle, toss 4 boneless,
skinless chicken breasts, about 150 g (5 oz) each,
in 2 tablespoons olive oil with 2 tablespoons chopped
tarragon and pepper. Cook the chicken breasts under
a preheated hot grill for 6–8 minutes on each side or
until cooked through. Meanwhile, cook 350 g (11½ oz)
tagliatelle for 9–12 minutes or according to the packet
instructions. Heat 1 tablespoon olive oil in a large
frying pan over a medium heat, add 4 chopped spring
onions and 12 quartered baby tomatoes and cook for
2 minutes. Slice the chicken breasts and add to the pan.
Drain the pasta and toss in the pan. Serve sprinkled
with 2 tablespoons toasted pine nuts. **Total cooking
time 20 minutes.**

182

bacon & chicken parcels

Serves **4**
Total cooking time **20 minutes**

4 small **chicken breasts**
125 g (4 oz) **smoked cheese**
 or **mozzarella cheese**,
 sliced
small bunch of **basil** (optional)
8 **smoked streaky bacon
 rashers**
2 tablespoons **olive** or
 vegetable oil
350 g (11½ oz) **fresh tomato
 and mascarpone pasta
 sauce** (or similar)
tagliatelle or **selection of
 vegetables**, to serve

Slice the chicken breasts almost in half horizontally,
then stuff each pocket with the sliced cheese and
2–3 basil leaves, if using. Wrap the bacon around the
chicken breasts to seal in the stuffing.

Heat the oil in a frying pan, add the chicken and cook
over a medium heat for 5–6 minutes on each side or
until the bacon is golden and the chicken is cooked
through. Pierce the chicken with a skewer or sharp
knife to check that the juices run clear, then remove
from the pan and set aside to rest for 2–3 minutes.

Meanwhile, gently warm the fresh sauce in the same
pan, scraping any bits from the bottom of the pan.
Serve the chicken parcels with cooked tagliatelle or
vegetables and the warmed sauce.

For chicken, ham & cheese parcels, lay out 4 soft
tortilla wraps and arrange 2 slices of wafer-thin ready-
cooked chicken breast and 50 g (2 oz) each of wafer-
thin smoked ham, smoked cheese or mozzarella and
drained and sliced roasted peppers in the centre of each
tortilla. Top each with 2–3 basil leaves (optional) and
fold the curved edges of each tortilla into the centre
4 times to create a square parcel. Heat a frying pan and
toast the parcels, 2 at a time, for 1–2 minutes on each
side. Serve hot with green salad. **Total cooking time
10 minutes.**

184

creamy chicken pasta

Serves **4**
Total cooking time **20 minutes**

250 g (8 oz) **penne**
4 tablespoons **olive oil**
500 g (1 lb) **skinless chicken breast fillets**, cut into thin strips
500 g (1 lb) **courgettes**, cut into thin slices
1 large **onion**, thinly sliced
2 teaspoons **crushed garlic**
4 tablespoons **pine nuts**
finely grated rind and juice of
  2 **lemons**
8 tablespoons chopped
  tarragon
200 ml (7 fl oz) **crème fraîche**
salt
grated **Parmesan cheese**,
  to serve

Cook the penne in a large saucepan of lightly salted boiling water for 8–10 minutes or according to the packet instructions, until 'al dente'.

Meanwhile, heat the oil in a large frying pan, add the chicken and cook for 3–4 minutes until starting to turn golden. Add the courgettes and onion and cook for a further 5 minutes until golden and the chicken is cooked through.

Add the garlic and pine nuts and cook, stirring, for 2 minutes, then add the lemon rind and juice, tarragon and crème fraîche and stir well until hot but not boiling.

Drain the pasta well, then add to the sauce and toss well to coat. Serve with grated Parmesan and a simple salad, if liked.

For creamy chicken & tarragon pan-fry, heat 2 tablespoons olive oil in a large frying pan, add 2 thinly sliced onions and 500 g (1 lb) thinly sliced skinless chicken breast fillets and cook for 5 minutes until golden and cooked through. Add 4 tablespoons chopped tarragon and 2 tablespoons white wine vinegar and cook for a further 1 minute, then stir in 200 ml (7 fl oz) crème fraîche and 2 teaspoons Dijon mustard. Serve hot. **Total cooking time 10 minutes.**

sticky lemon chicken noodles

Serves **4**
Total cooking time **10 minutes**

2 tablespoons **vegetable oil**
300 g (10 oz) **skinless chicken breast fillets**, cut into thin strips
200 g (7 oz) **Tenderstem broccoli**
2 **garlic cloves**, crushed
2 teaspoons peeled and finely grated **fresh root ginger**
1 **red chilli**, finely chopped
finely grated rind and juice of **1 lemon**
1 tablespoon **clear honey**
2 teaspoons **light soy sauce**
300 g (10 oz) **ready-cooked egg noodles**
handful of **roasted cashew nuts**

Heat a wok until smoking hot, then pour in the oil, swirl around the pan and add the chicken. Cook for 1 minute, then add the broccoli and stir-fry for 5 minutes until the chicken is nearly cooked through.

Add the garlic, ginger and chilli to the wok and cook for a further 1 minute. Then add the lemon rind and juice, the honey and soy sauce and toss around the pan.

Stir in the noodles and a splash of water and cook until heated through. Divide between 4 serving bowls, scatter over the cashew nuts and serve.

For roasted lemon chicken with broccoli, mix together 1 teaspoon ground cumin, 1 teaspoon clear honey, 1 crushed garlic clove and 3 tablespoons olive oil. Stir in the finely grated rind of 1 lemon and a squeeze of lemon juice and season to taste. Place 4 boneless, skinless chicken breasts and 200 g (7 oz) Tenderstem broccoli in a roasting tin. Pour over the lemon mixture and toss well. Place in a preheated oven, 200°C (400°F), Gas Mark 6, for 20 minutes or until the chicken is cooked through. Sprinkle over some sesame seeds and serve with boiled rice. **Total cooking time 20 minutes.**

sticky soy-glazed drumsticks

Serves **4**

Total cooking time **30 minutes**

8 **chicken drumsticks**
2 tablespoons **clear honey**
2 tablespoons **olive oil**
2 tablespoons **dark soy sauce**
1 teaspoon **tomato purée**
1 tablespoon **Dijon mustard**
chopped **parsley**, to garnish

Put the drumsticks on a board and make 4 deep slashes in each one along the thick part of the meat, cutting down to the bone on both sides.

Mix together the honey, oil, soy sauce, tomato purée and mustard in a large bowl. Toss the drumsticks in the glaze, turning to cover the meat well.

Transfer the drumsticks to a roasting tin and roast in the top of a preheated oven, 220°C (425°F), Gas Mark 7, for 20–25 minutes or until the chicken is cooked through. Garnish with parsley and serve with boiled rice and a salad, if liked.

For sticky chilli soy-glazed chicken breasts, mix together the honey, oil, soy sauce, tomato purée and mustard as above to make the glaze and add 1 finely chopped small red chilli. Coat 4 boneless, skinless chicken breasts, each about 125 g (4 oz), in the glaze. Heat 1 tablespoon olive oil in a large, heavy-based frying pan and cook the chicken over a medium-high heat for 15 minutes, turning it frequently and reducing the heat a little if the glaze begins to catch on the base of the pan, until the chicken is cooked through. Slice the cooked chicken and serve fanned on a plate, with boiled rice and salad. **Total cooking time 20 minutes.**

stir-fried lemon chicken

Serves **2**
Total cooking time **20 minutes**

1 tablespoon **groundnut oil**
250 (8 oz) **skinless chicken
  breast fillets**, sliced
125 g (4 oz) **broccoli florets**
1 small **red pepper**, roughly
  chopped
2 **spring onions**, thickly sliced
50 g (2 oz) **unsalted cashew
  nuts**
1 tablespoon **cornflour**
125 ml (4 fl oz) cold **water**
2 tablespoons **lemon juice**
1½ tablespoons **clear honey**
2 tablespoons **light soy sauce**

Heat the oil in a large wok or frying pan, add the chicken and cook over a medium-high heat for 3–4 minutes, until golden. Using a slotted spoon, transfer to a plate and set aside.

Return the pan to the heat and add the broccoli, red pepper and spring onions. Stir-fry for 3–4 minutes until softened.

Meanwhile, place a small pan over a medium-low heat and toast the cashew nuts for 3–4 minutes, shaking the pan occasionally, until golden. Remove from the heat.

Blend the cornflour in a small bowl with 1 tablespoon of the water, then mix in the remaining water plus the lemon juice, honey and soy sauce. Add to the vegetables along with the cashew nuts. Reduce the heat to medium-low and return the chicken to the pan. Simmer for 2–3 minutes until the chicken is cooked through and the sauce hot and thickened. Serve immediately, with steamed rice or noodles, if liked.

For crunchy lemon chicken salad, place 2 teaspoons grated lemon rind in a dish with 75 g (3 oz) breadcrumbs. Place 50 g (2 oz) plain flour in a second dish and 1 beaten egg in a third. Dip 250 g (8 oz) chicken mini-fillets first in the flour, then the egg and finally the breadcrumbs until coated. Heat 2 tablespoons groundnut oil in a frying pan and cook the mini-fillets for 7–8 minutes, turning occasionally, until golden and cooked through. Serve with mixed salad leaves, sprinkled with 2 tablespoons toasted cashew nuts and 1 thinly sliced spring onion, and desired dressing. **Total cooking time 10 minutes.**

chicken & chorizo jambalaya

Serves **4**
Total cooking time **30 minutes**

175 g (6 oz) **long-grain rice**
1 tablespoon **olive oil**
250 g (8 oz) piece of **chorizo sausage**, cut into chunky slices
1 **onion**, chopped
375 g (12 oz) **skinless chicken breast fillets**, cut into chunks
1 **red pepper**, cored, deseeded and cut into chunks
1 **green pepper**, cored, deseeded and cut into chunks
1 **yellow pepper**, cored, deseeded and cut into chunks
2 **celery sticks**, chopped
1 tablespoon **cornflour**, mixed to a paste with 2 tablespoons cold water
600 ml (1 pint) **chicken stock**
400 g (13 oz) can **chopped tomatoes**
salt and **pepper**
4 tablespoons chopped **parsley**, to garnish

Cook the rice in a saucepan of lightly salted water for 15 minutes until tender, then drain.

Meanwhile, heat the oil in a large, heavy-based frying pan, add the chorizo, onion and chicken and cook over a medium heat, for 10 minutes, stirring occasionally, until browned and cooked through. Add the peppers and celery and cook, for a further 5 minutes, stirring occasionally.

Blend the measurement water with the cornflour, then stir into the stock, add to the pan with the tomatoes and bring to the boil. Reduce the heat and simmer for 5 minutes before adding the cooked rice. Season generously with pepper.

Serve garnished with the parsley, accompanied by crusty bread and salad, if liked.

For Creole-style jambalaya, heat 1 tablespoon olive oil in a large saucepan, add 1 chopped onion and cook over a medium heat for 5 minutes, stirring occasionally. Add 200 g (7 oz) sliced chorizo sausage, 4 chunkily shredded ready-cooked chicken breasts and 1 teaspoon Creole spice mix. Cook for 1 minute, then add a 350 g (11½ oz) tub fresh tomato sauce, 100 ml (3½ fl oz) chicken stock and 600 g (1 lb 5 oz) ready-cooked egg-fried rice. Stir, heat through, season and serve. **Total cooking time 10 minutes.**

herb-stuffed chicken breasts

Serves **4**
Total cooking time **30 minutes**

4 **boneless, skinless chicken breasts**
150 g (5 oz) **cream cheese**
2 **garlic cloves**, crushed
½ tablespoon chopped **parsley**
½ tablespoon chopped **chives**
10 slices of **Parma ham**
½ tablespoon **vegetable oil**, for oiling
2 **leeks**, finely sliced
300 ml (½ pint) **fromage frais**
salt and **pepper**
crisp green salad, to serve

Using a sharp knife, make a slit in the side of each chicken breast, to make a little pocket.

Mix together the cream cheese, garlic, herbs and some salt and pepper in a bowl.

Lay 2 slices of the Parma ham on a chopping board and place 1 of the chicken breasts on top. Spoon one-quarter of the cream cheese mixture into the chicken breast, then wrap around the Parma ham to seal the pocket. Repeat with the remaining ham, cream cheese and chicken to make 4 parcels. Place in a roasting tin and bake in a preheated oven, 200°C (400°F), Gas Mark 6, for 20 minutes or until cooked through.

Meanwhile, chop the remaining Parma ham and fry in a lightly oiled frying pan over a medium heat for 1–2 minutes. Add the leeks and stir-fry for 2–3 minutes, then stir in the fromage frais and some salt and pepper.

Serve the chicken with a crisp green salad and the bacon and leek sauce.

For herby chicken pittas, mix 150 g (5 oz) cream cheese with 2 tablespoons chopped fresh herbs of your choice. Toast 4 pitta breads for 2–3 minutes on each side, then cut along the long side to open like a pocket. Spread the inside of each pitta bread with the cream cheese. Slice 3 ready-cooked chicken breasts, then stuff each pitta bread with one-quarter of the chicken, 30 g (1¼ oz) crisp salad leaves and a dollop of mango sauce. **Total cooking time 10 minutes.**

chicken & ham cobbler

Serves **4**
Total cooking time **30 minutes**

2 tablespoons **butter**

2 **leeks**, sliced

300 g (10 oz) **skinless chicken thigh fillets**, diced

150 g (5 oz) piece of **ham**, cut into small chunks

150 ml (¼ pint) hot **chicken stock**

100 ml (3½ fl oz) **crème fraîche**

150 g (5 oz) **plain flour**

1 tablespoon **baking powder**

2 tablespoons **olive oil**

150 ml (¼ pint) **milk**

2 tablespoons **mixed herbs**, such as parsley, thyme, chives, finely chopped

25 g (1 oz) **Cheddar cheese**, grated

salt and **pepper**

Melt the butter in a shallow, flameproof casserole dish, add the leeks and cook for 3 minutes until softened. Add the chicken and cook for 2 minutes until lightly browned all over. Stir in the ham, stock and crème fraîche, then season to taste.

Mix the flour and baking powder in a bowl, then pour in the oil and milk. Mix gently, season well and stir in the herbs and cheese.

Arrange spoonfuls of the dough on top of the chicken mixture, leaving a little space between each spoonful. Place in a preheated oven, 220°C (425°F), Gas Mark 7, for 15–20 minutes until the topping is lightly browned and the chicken is cooked through.

For creamy chicken & ham pasta, cook 400 g (13 oz) quick-cook spaghetti in a large saucepan of lightly salted boiling water according to the packet instructions, adding 1 finely sliced leek for the last 5 minutes of cooking. Drain and return the pasta and leek to the pan. Stir in 2 shredded ready-cooked chicken breasts and 4 slices of ham, torn into strips. Season well, add 4 tablespoons crème fraîche, then scatter with chopped parsley to serve. **Total cooking time 10 minutes.**

cajun chicken quinoa with apricots

Serves **4**
Total cooking time **30 minutes**

600 ml (1 pint) **chicken stock**
100 g (3½ oz) **quinoa**
100 g (3½ oz) **ready-to-eat dried apricots**, roughly chopped
3 **skinless chicken breast fillets**, thinly sliced
2 teaspoons **Cajun spice mix**
2 tablespoons **olive oil**
2 **red onions**, cut into slim wedges
2 bunches of **spring onions**, roughly chopped
6 tablespoons chopped **fresh coriander**
Greek yogurt, to serve

Place the stock in a saucepan and bring to the boil, add the quinoa, then simmer for 10 minutes. Stir in the apricots and cook for a further 5 minutes.

Meanwhile, toss the chicken with the Cajun spice in a bowl to coat. Heat the oil in a large, heavy-based frying pan, add the chicken and onion wedges and cook over a medium-high heat for 10 minutes, stirring frequently, until the chicken is well browned and cooked through. Add the spring onions and cook for a further 1 minute.

Drain the quinoa and apricots, then add to the chicken mixture and toss well to mix. Toss in the chopped coriander and serve with spoonfuls of Greek yogurt, with crusty bread, if liked.

For chicken with fresh apricot lentils, heat 1 tablespoon olive oil in a large frying pan and cook 1 finely chopped red onion over a medium heat for 5 minutes, stirring frequently. Pour in 4 tablespoons red wine vinegar and cook for 30 seconds. Add 250 g (8 oz) ready-cooked Puy lentils, 4 fresh stoned apricots cut into chunks and 4 tablespoons each of chopped fresh coriander and mint. Add 600 g (1¼ lb) shredded ready-cooked chicken breast and heat through for 1 minute. To serve, stir in 50 g (2 oz) rocket leaves. **Total cooking time 10 minutes.**

thai meatballs with noodles

Serves **4**
Total cooking time **20 minutes**

500 g (1 lb) **minced chicken**
3 **spring onions**, finely diced
2 **garlic cloves**, finely diced
1 **red chilli**, deseeded and
 finely diced
5 cm (2 inch) piece of **fresh
 root ginger**, peeled and
 finely diced
600 ml (1 pint) **chicken stock**
350 g (11½ oz) **rice noodles**
300 g (10 oz) **ready-made
 tomato sauce**, heated
fresh coriander leaves, to
 garnish

Mix together the minced chicken, spring onions, garlic, chilli and ginger. Using wet hands, divide the chicken mixture into 16 portions and roll into balls.

Pour the stock into a large pan and bring to the boil. Add the meatballs and simmer for 10 minutes.

Meanwhile, cook the rice noodles according to the packet instructions, then drain and serve with the meatballs and tomato sauce, garnished with the coriander leaves.

For Thai chicken curry with noodles, heat 1 tablespoon vegetable oil in a wok over a high heat, add 2 diced shallots and 1 diced lemon grass stick and cook for 1–2 minutes. Stir in 3–4 teaspoons red Thai curry paste and cook for 1 minute, stirring. Add 600 g (1 lb 5 oz) skinless chicken breast fillets, cut into bite-sized pieces, and stir-fry for 5–6 minutes. Add ½ tablespoon fish sauce, 1 teaspoon brown sugar and a couple of lime leaves with a 400 ml (14 fl oz) can of coconut milk. Bring to a simmer and cook for 15 minutes until the chicken is cooked through. Cook 150 g (5 oz) rice noodles according to the packet instructions. Stir a small handful of roughly torn coriander leaves into the curry and serve with the rice noodles. **Total cooking time 30 minutes.**

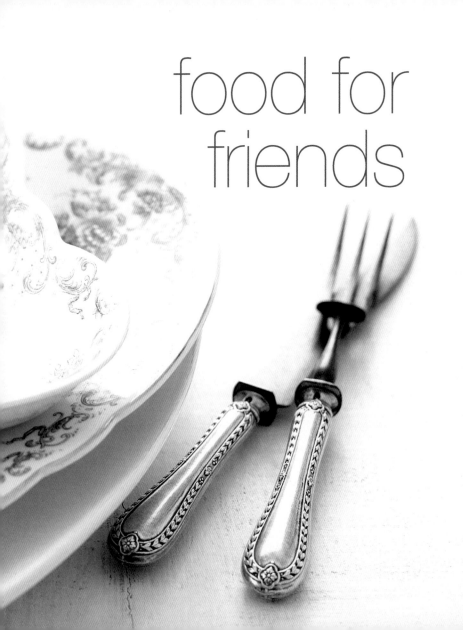

food for
friends

chicken & goats' cheese tarts

Serves **4**
Total cooking time **30 minutes**

375 g (12 oz) **ready-rolled
  puff pastry**, cut into 4 equal
  rectangles
2 tablespoons **olive oil**
250 g (8 oz) **skinless chicken
  breast fillets**, diced
200 g (7 oz) **spinach leaves**
½ teaspoon **ground nutmeg**
1 teaspoon **mustard seeds**
8 tablespoons **ready-made
  red** or **white onion chutney**
8 thick slices of **rinded goats'
  cheese**
salt and **pepper**

Put the 4 pastry sheets on a large baking sheet and
prick all over with a fork.

Heat the oil in a large, heavy-based frying pan and cook
the chicken over a high heat for 3 minutes. Add the
spinach leaves, toss and cook for 1 minute until wilted.
Remove from the heat, add the nutmeg and mustard
seeds and season with a little salt and pepper, tossing
well to coat.

Drain the mixture if necessary, then spoon evenly on
to the 4 sheets of pastry to within 2.5 cm (1 inch) of
the edges. Spoon 2 tablespoons of onion chutney over
the top of each and put the goats' cheese on top. Bake
in a preheated oven, 220°C (425°F), Gas Mark 7, for
20 minutes until puffed and golden. Serve with a salad.

For chicken, spinach & goats' cheese tarts, heat
1 tablespoon olive oil and 15 g (½ oz) butter in a large,
heavy-based frying pan and cook 250 g (8 oz) diced
skinless chicken breast fillets for 5 minutes. Add 100 g
(3½ oz) spinach leaves and toss and stir for 2 minutes.
Add ½ teaspoon ground nutmeg and season well. Chop
50 g (2 oz) rinded goats' cheese into small cubes and
stir into the chicken and spinach. Spoon the mixture into
4 ready-made pastry cases and serve with salad. **Total
cooking time 10 minutes.**

sesame chicken & noodles

Serves **4**
Total cooking time **20 minutes**

350 g (11½ oz) **skinless chicken breast** or **thigh fillets**, cut into thin strips
2 teaspoons **cornflour**
1 tablespoon **dark soy sauce**
1½ tablespoons **sesame oil**
2 teaspoons **sesame seeds**, plus extra to serve
2 teaspoons **clear honey**
2 tablespoons **vegetable oil**
1 **onion**, thinly sliced
1 **red pepper**, cored, deseeded and thinly sliced
250 g (8 oz) **courgettes**, thinly sliced
1 tablespoon peeled and finely chopped **fresh root ginger** (optional)
400 g (13 oz) **dried medium egg noodles**
125 ml (4 fl oz) **water**

Mix the chicken with the cornflour, soy sauce, 1 tablespoon of the sesame oil, the sesame seeds and honey. Leave to marinate.

Heat the vegetable oil in a large frying pan or wok, add the onion and red pepper and cook for 3–4 minutes, until slightly softened. Add the courgettes and ginger, if using, and cook for a further 4–5 minutes, stirring frequently, until slightly softened.

Meanwhile, bring a large saucepan of water to the boil, add the egg noodles and immediately remove from the heat. Cover and set aside for 4–5 minutes, until tender. Alternatively, cook according to the packet instructions. Drain and refresh under cold running water, then toss in the remaining sesame oil.

Add the chicken and its marinade to the vegetables and cook gently for 1–2 minutes to seal. Stir in the measurement water and simmer for 2–3 minutes, until the chicken is cooked through and the sauce thickened.

Stir the noodles into the pan and cook for 1–2 minutes until hot, then heap into bowls and serve sprinkled with extra sesame seeds.

For sesame chicken noodle salad, cook and cool 400 g (13 oz) dried medium egg noodles, as above. Toss with 1 sliced red pepper, 2 sliced spring onions, 150 g (5 oz) bean sprouts and 250 g (8 oz) ready-cooked chicken strips. Mix 2 tablespoons vegetable and 1½ tablespoons sesame oils, 2 teaspoons honey, 1 tablespoon dark soy sauce and 1 teaspoon finely grated fresh root ginger, then toss into the noodles. Sprinkle with sesame seeds. **Total cooking time 10 minutes.**

cacciatore-style chicken pasta

Serves **4**
Total cooking time **25 minutes**

3 tablespoons **olive oil**
1 **red onion**, thinly sliced
2 **garlic cloves**, chopped
400 g (13 oz) **skinless
  chicken breast fillets**, thinly
  sliced
90 g (3¼ oz) **salami**, thinly
  sliced and halved
125 ml (4 fl oz) **red wine**
2 **rosemary sprigs**, leaves
  chopped
2 x 400 g (13 oz) cans **cherry
  tomatoes**
75 g (3 oz) **green olives**,
  pitted (optional)
400 g (13 oz) **pasta**, such as
  fusilli
salt and **pepper**

Heat the oil in a large frying pan and cook the onion
and garlic over a medium-high heat for 4–5 minutes
until slightly softened. Add the chicken and salami and
cook for a further 3–4 minutes until lightly golden.

Pour the wine into the pan and simmer until completely
evaporated. Add the rosemary, tomatoes and olives, if
using, and simmer for 8–10 minutes until thickened
slightly. Season to taste.

Meanwhile, cook the pasta in a large pan of lightly
salted boiling water for about 11 minutes, or according
to the packet instructions, until 'al dente'. Drain and heap
into 4 serving bowls. Top with the sauce and serve.

For cacciatore chicken & salami ciabatta, heat
2 tablespoons olive oil in a frying pan and fry 400 g
(13 oz) chicken mini-fillets over a medium-high heat
for 8 minutes, turning occasionally, or until cooked
through and golden. Transfer to a plate and set aside.
Meanwhile, cut 1 large ciabatta loaf into 8 sandwich
slices. Divide 90 g (3¼ oz) sliced salami between
4 pieces of the bread. Slice 150 g (5 oz) cherry
tomatoes, 50 g (2 oz) pitted green olives and ½ small
red onion. Put a little of each on top of the salami, then
add some of the chicken fillets and a small handful
of rocket. Cover with the remaining bread and serve.
Total cooking time 10 minutes.

chicken fettuccine alfredo

Serves **4**
Total cooking time **20 minutes**

2 **boneless, skinless chicken breasts**
400 g (13 oz) **fettuccine**
25 g (1 oz) **butter**
125 ml (4 fl oz) **single cream**
50 g (2 oz) **Parmesan cheese**, grated
salt and **pepper**
finely sliced **chives**, to garnish

Place the chicken breasts in a small pan, pour over enough water to cover and simmer for 12–15 minutes or until just cooked through.

Meanwhile, cook the pasta in a large saucepan of salted boiling water according to the packet instructions until 'al dente'.

Melt the butter in a separate saucepan, stir in the cream and simmer for 1–2 minutes, then season well. Using a fork, break the chicken into bite-sized pieces.

Drain the pasta, reserving a little of the cooking water, and return to the pan. Toss through the chicken, creamy sauce and Parmesan, adding a little cooking water to loosen if needed. Season well.

Spoon into 4 serving bowls and serve sprinkled with the chives.

For quick chicken spaghetti alfredo, cook 400 g (13 oz) quick-cook spaghetti and the cream sauce as above. Drain the pasta, reserving a little of the cooking water, and return to the pan. Toss through 2 ready-cooked roast chicken breasts, skin discarded and torn into shreds, the sauce and Parmesan as above. Serve immediately. **Total cooking time 10 minutes.**

chicken & olive couscous

Serves **4**
Total cooking time **10 minutes**

4 tablespoons **olive oil**
½ **lemon** (rind and flesh),
   finely chopped
1 tablespoon **clear honey**
½ teaspoon **ground cumin**
1 **garlic clove**, crushed
300 g (10 oz) **couscous**
300 ml (½ pint) hot **chicken
   stock**
400 g (13 oz) can **chickpeas**,
   rinsed and drained
50 g (2 oz) **green olives**,
   pitted
2 **ready-cooked chicken
   breasts**, sliced
handful each of **fresh
   coriander** and **mint**,
   chopped
salt and **pepper**

Heat the oil and lemon in a saucepan and cook over a gentle heat for about 2 minutes until the lemon is soft.

Stir in the honey, cumin and garlic and heat through. Stir in the couscous, stock, chickpeas, olives and chicken.

Remove from the heat, cover and leave to stand for 5 minutes until the couscous is tender. Fluff up with a fork and stir in the coriander and mint. Season to taste and serve immediately.

For cumin-dusted chicken breasts with spicy olive couscous, heat 2 tablespoons olive oil in a frying pan. Dust 4 small boneless, skinless chicken breasts with 1 teaspoon ground cumin, season and cook for 5 minutes on each side until just cooked through. Stir in 1 crushed garlic clove and 2 teaspoons harissa or chilli paste. Add 250 g (8 oz) couscous, 300 ml (½ pint) hot chicken stock and 50 g (2 oz) green olives. Cover and leave to stand for 5 minutes until the couscous is tender. Fluff up with a fork and stir in a handful each of chopped mint and fresh coriander and the grated rind and juice of ½ lemon. **Total cooking time 20 minutes.**

quick coq au vin

Serves **4**
Total cooking time **30 minutes**

2 tablespoons **olive oil**
8 **chicken drumsticks**
8 **streaky bacon rashers**,
  roughly chopped
8 **whole shallots**
250 g (8 oz) **chestnut
  mushrooms**, halved
1 tablespoon **plain flour**
2 tablespoons **thyme leaves**
300 ml (½ pint) **red wine**
450 ml (¾ pint) **rich chicken
  stock**
thyme sprigs, to garnish
mashed potatoes, to serve

Heat the oil in a large, heavy-based frying pan, add the drumsticks and bacon and cook over a high heat for 5 minutes. Add the shallots and mushrooms and cook for a further 5 minutes, turning the chicken and shallots, until golden all over. Add the flour and toss to coat, then add the thyme.

Pour in the wine and stock and bring to the boil, stirring continually to distribute the flour evenly within the sauce. Reduce the heat and simmer, uncovered, for 15 minutes until the chicken is cooked through.

Garnish the coq au vin with thyme sprigs and serve ladled on to hot mashed potatoes in 4 warmed serving bowls.

For chicken, mushroom & red wine soup with croutons, heat 1 tablespoon olive oil in a pan and cook 175 g (6 oz) diced skinless chicken breast fillets with 1 chopped onion and 125 g (4 oz) roughly chopped mushrooms over a high heat for 5 minutes until the chicken is cooked through. Meanwhile, make 40 g (1¾ oz) red wine sauce according to the packet instructions and add to the chicken with 300 ml (½ pint) chicken stock. Bring to the boil, ladle into warmed serving bowls and serve scattered with ready-made croutons. **Total cooking time 10 minutes.**

chicken & brie puff pie

Serves **4**
Total cooking time **20 minutes**

320 g (10¾ oz) **ready-rolled
sheet of puff pastry**
1 small **egg**, beaten
1 tablespoon **olive oil**
2 **leeks**, chopped
150 g (5 oz) **baby button
mushrooms**, halved
350 g (11½ oz) **ready-cooked
chicken**, diced
100 g (3½ oz) **Brie cheese**,
sliced
4 slices of **prosciutto**, cut into
strips
1 teaspoon chopped **thyme
leaves** (optional)
4 tablespoons **half-fat crème
fraîche**
salt and **pepper**

Line a baking sheet with baking paper. Unroll the
pastry, place a pie dish on it upside down and cut
around it. Place the pastry on the prepared sheet, brush
with beaten egg and bake in a preheated oven, 200°C
(400°F), Gas Mark 6, for about 10 minutes until puffed
up and pale golden.

Meanwhile, heat the oil in a large frying pan, add the
leeks and cook for 3–4 minutes until softened. Add the
mushrooms and cook for a further 3–4 minutes until
soft and golden. Add the remaining ingredients, season
to taste and cook until the chicken is hot.

Put the filling into the pie dish, top with the pastry lid
and return to the oven for 3–4 minutes or until the pastry
is golden and crisp.

For chicken, Brie & thyme melts, split 1 baguette in
half lengthways and then widthways to make 4 equal
pieces. Spread each cut side with 2 tablespoons onion
chutney. Take 200 g (7 oz) chunky sliced ready-cooked
chicken, 150 g (5 oz) sliced Brie, 150 g (5 oz) halved
cherry tomatoes and 1 teaspoon thyme leaves and
place equal amounts of each on the bread. Drizzle each
slice with ½ teaspoon olive oil, place on a rack and slide
under a preheated medium-hot grill for 5–6 minutes
until melted and golden. Serve with rocket leaves.
Total cooking time 10 minutes.

feta-stuffed chicken with chilli

Serves **4**
Total cooking time **30 minutes**

200 g (7 oz) **feta cheese**,
   crumbled
1 **red chilli**, deseeded and
   chopped
2 teaspoons rinsed **capers**
1 teaspoon grated **lemon** rind
70 g (2¾ oz) **pitted olives**,
   sliced
2 tablespoons chopped **fresh
   coriander** or **parsley**
2 tablespoons **olive oil**
4 **boneless chicken breasts**,
   skin on
4 **lemon** wedges
2 **Romano peppers**, halved
   lengthways and deseeded
250 g (8 oz) **wholewheat
   couscous**
salt and **pepper**

Place the feta in a small bowl and add the chilli, capers,
lemon rind, olives, coriander or parsley and half the
olive oil. Season generously with salt and pepper.

Cut a pocket in the side of each chicken breast and
fill with half the feta mixture. Place skin side up in an
ovenproof dish with the lemon wedges and Romano
peppers.

Drizzle over the remaining olive oil and place in a
preheated oven, 220°C (425°F), Gas Mark 7, for about
20 minutes until the chicken is cooked and golden.

Meanwhile, cook the couscous according to the
packet instructions, fluff up with a fork and fold in the
remaining feta mixture. Spoon on to plates and serve
with the stuffed chicken, roasted peppers and lemon
wedges.

For chilli chicken & feta rolls, place 300 g (10 oz)
sliced ready-cooked chicken breasts in a large bowl
with the feta, chilli, capers, olives and coriander from the
main recipe. Add 1 tablespoon olive oil, 2 teaspoons
lemon juice, 70 g (2¾ oz) rocket leaves and a pinch
of salt and pepper. Toss to combine, then heap on to
4 large, soft flour tortillas. Roll up the tortillas and toast
them on a hot ridged griddle pan for 4–5 minutes,
turning occasionally, until warm and charred. Cut in half
diagonally and serve with a tabbouleh salad or steamed
wholewheat couscous for a more substantial meal.
Total cooking time 10 minutes.

chicken parmigiana with fusilli

Serves **4**
Total cooking time **20 minutes**

100 g (3½ oz) **fresh white breadcrumbs**
25 g (1 oz) **Parmesan cheese**, grated
4 tablespoons **olive oil**, plus extra for greasing
4 small **boneless, skinless chicken breasts**
75 g (3 oz) **mozzarella cheese**, cut into 4 slices
300 g (10 oz) **fusilli lunghi**
250 ml (8 fl oz) **shop-bought tomato pasta sauce**
salt and **pepper**
green salad, to serve

Mix together the breadcrumbs and Parmesan on a large plate and season. Rub about 2 teaspoons of the oil over each chicken breast, press down with your palm to flatten a little, then dip in the breadcrumb mixture until coated all over. Place on a lightly greased grill pan.

Drizzle with a little more oil, then cook under a preheated hot grill for 10 minutes, turning once, until golden and cooked through. Top each chicken breast with a slice of mozzarella and cook for a further 2 minutes or until the cheese has melted.

Meanwhile, cook the pasta in a large saucepan of salted boiling water according to the packet instructions until 'al dente'. Heat the tomato pasta sauce in a small saucepan. Drain the pasta and toss through the sauce. Cut each chicken breast in half. Spoon into serving bowls and top with the grilled chicken. Serve with green salad.

For easy chicken, mozzarella & tomato spaghetti,
heat 1 tablespoon olive oil in a wok or large frying pan, add 300 g (10 oz) stir-fry chicken strips and stir-fry for 7 minutes or until just cooked through. Pour over 250 ml (8 fl oz) shop-bought tomato pasta sauce and simmer for 1–2 minutes. Meanwhile, cook 400 g (13 oz) spaghetti according to the packet instructions until 'al dente'. Drain and return to the pan. Cut 75 g (3 oz) mozzarella cheese into small chunks and stir through the pasta with the chicken sauce. Serve immediately. **Total cooking time 10 minutes.**

baked chicken with gremolata

Serves **4**

Total cooking time **20 minutes**

500 g (1 lb) **new potatoes**,
   thinly sliced

3 tablespoons **olive oil**

4 **boneless, skinless chicken
   breasts**, about 150 g (5 oz)
   each

150 g (5 oz) **asparagus**,
   trimmed

salt and **pepper**

Gremolata

1 **garlic clove**, finely chopped

finely grated rind of 1 **lemon**

large handful of chopped
   parsley

Toss the potatoes with 2 tablespoons of the oil and place in a large, shallow roasting tin. Place in a preheated oven, 200°C (400°F), Gas Mark 6, for 5 minutes, then arrange the chicken breasts on top and drizzle over a little more oil. Season well and return to the oven for a further 10 minutes.

Arrange the asparagus spears in the tin, pour over any remaining oil and return to the oven for a further 5 minutes until the chicken and potatoes are golden and cooked through.

Meanwhile, make the gremolata. Mix together the garlic, lemon rind and parsley. Scatter over the chicken and vegetables before serving.

For chicken, asparagus & gremolata frittata, heat 2 tablespoons olive oil in a large, nonstick frying pan. Add 100 g (3½ oz) asparagus tips and 1 crushed garlic clove and cook for 5 minutes until tender. Mix 1 ready-cooked chicken breast, cut into bite-sized pieces, with 6 beaten eggs, the finely grated rind of 1 lemon and a handful of chopped parsley. Season to taste and pour into the pan, mix gently together, then cook over a low heat for 15 minutes or until the egg is cooked through. **Total cooking time 30 minutes.**

chicken with mustard sauce

Serves **4**

Total cooking time **20 minutes**

1 tablespoon **olive oil**

15 g (½ oz) **butter**

4 **boneless, skinless chicken breasts**, about 150 g (5 oz) each

200 ml (7 fl oz) **crème fraîche**

1 tablespoon **wholegrain mustard**

1 teaspoon **English mustard**

1 teaspoon **Dijon mustard**

3 tablespoons chopped **parsley**

pepper

To serve

green beans

new potatoes

Heat the oil and butter in a large, heavy-based frying pan and cook the chicken over a high heat for 20 minutes, turning once, or until golden and cooked through. Use a fish slice to remove the chicken from the pan and keep it warm.

Add the crème fraîche to the pan with the mustards and stir for 2–3 minutes until warm but not boiled. Stir in the chopped parsley and season generously with pepper. Serve the chicken on warmed serving plates and spoon the sauce over. Serve with green beans and buttered new potatoes.

For creamy chicken pan-fry with hot mustard sauce, heat 25 g (1 oz) butter in a pan and cook 375 g (12 oz) diced skinless chicken breast fillets over a high heat for 7–8 minutes or until golden and cooked through. Add 1 tablespoon Dijon mustard, 2 teaspoons English mustard and 1 teaspoon wholegrain mustard. Stir well, then add 150 ml (¼ pint) double cream. Stir and heat for 2 minutes until piping hot. Spoon on to warmed serving plates and garnish with parsley sprigs. **Total cooking time 10 minutes.**

chicken & winter vegetable roast

Serves **4**

Total cooking time **30 minutes**

4 tablespoons **olive oil**

4 **boneless chicken breasts**,
  skin on

400 g (13 oz) small **waxy
  potatoes**, halved

400 g (13 oz) **carrots**,
  quartered

400 g (13 oz) **parsnips**, cored
  and quartered

4 **banana shallots**, quartered

6 small **garlic cloves**

2 **thyme sprigs**

rosemary sprig

salt and **pepper**

Heat half the oil in a large frying pan over a medium-high heat, add the chicken, skin side down, and cook without moving for 7–8 minutes, until the skin is really crisp and golden.

Meanwhile, parboil the potatoes in a large saucepan of salted boiling water for 6–7 minutes, adding the carrots and parsnips for the final 3 minutes. They should all be starting to soften.

Drain well and place in a large roasting tin. Add the shallots, garlic, herbs and remaining oil, season generously and toss well. Nestle the chicken in with the vegetables, skin side up.

Roast in a preheated oven, 220°C (425°F), Gas Mark 7, for about 20 minutes until the chicken is cooked through and the vegetables are golden. Serve with steamed kale, if liked.

For pan-fried chicken with roasted vegetables,
tip a 480 g (15¼ oz) bag winter vegetable mix, such as sprouts, carrots and broccoli, into a large roasting tin with 500 g (1 lb) halved miniature new potatoes. Toss with 3 tablespoons olive oil, 2 thyme sprigs and a generous pinch of salt and pepper. Roast in a preheated oven, 230°C (450°F), Gas Mark 8, for 18 minutes, shaking the pan occasionally, until tender and golden. Meanwhile, heat 2 tablespoons olive oil in a large frying pan and cook 4 seasoned boneless chicken breasts, skin side down, for 8–10 minutes until really golden. Turn the chicken and cook for a further 3–5 minutes or until the juices run clear. Serve the chicken with the roasted vegetables. **Total cooking time 20 minutes.**

chicken & mushroom rice

Serves **4**

Total cooking time **10 minutes**

50 g (2 oz) **butter**

3 **spring onions**, sliced

2 **ready-cooked roast chicken breasts**, sliced or shredded

500 g (1 lb) **ready-cooked long-grain and wild rice mixture**

290 g (9¾ oz) **jar mushroom antipasti**, drained

4 tablespoons **crème fraîche**

salt and **pepper**

Melt the butter in a large frying pan, add the spring onions and cook over a medium heat for 2–3 minutes until softened. Add the chicken, rice and all but a small handful of the mushrooms. Stir-fry for 3–4 minutes, until piping hot.

Add the crème fraîche, season to taste and stir occasionally for about 2 minutes until hot and creamy. Spoon into shallow bowls and serve immediately, topped with the reserved mushrooms.

For chicken & mushroom fried rice, cook 350 g (11½ oz) quick-cook long-grain rice for 8–9 minutes, or according to the packet instructions, until just tender. Drain well. Heat 2 tablespoons vegetable oil in a large frying pan or wok, add 3 sliced spring onions and 2 chopped garlic cloves and fry for 2–3 minutes. Add 200 g (7 oz) diced chestnut mushrooms and the shredded chicken from the main recipe and stir-fry for 3–4 minutes until soft and golden. Increase the heat slightly and add the rice and 75 g (3 oz) defrosted peas. Stir-fry for 3–4 minutes until hot and lightly golden. Season to taste, then spoon into bowls and serve with soy sauce. **Total cooking time 20 minutes.**

linguine with marsala chicken

Serves **4**
Total cooking time **30 minutes**

3 tablespoons **olive oil**
2 **boneless chicken breasts**
1 **shallot**, finely sliced
150 ml (¼ pint) **Marsala**
150 ml (¼ pint) hot **chicken stock**
1 **sage leaf**, finely chopped
100 ml (3½ fl oz) **double cream**
200 g (7 oz) **chestnut mushrooms**, halved if large
400 g (13 oz) **linguine**
salt and **pepper**
chopped **flat leaf parsley**, to garnish

Heat 1 tablespoon of the oil in a frying pan. Season the chicken breasts well and then add to the pan and cook for 5–7 minutes on each side or until golden and cooked through.

Meanwhile, heat 1 tablespoon of the oil in a saucepan, add the shallot and cook over a low heat for a couple of minutes until softened. Pour over the Marsala, increase the heat to high and cook for a couple of minutes until reduced and slightly syrupy. Add the stock and sage and simmer for a further 5 minutes. Stir in the cream, season well and keep warm.

Cut the chicken into slices and add to the sauce. Add the remaining oil to the frying pan and cook the mushrooms for 3–5 minutes until golden all over, then stir into the sauce.

Meanwhile, cook the pasta in a large pan of salted boiling water according to the packet instructions. Drain, reserving a little of the cooking water, and return to the pan. Toss through the sauce, adding cooking water to loosen if needed. Season and sprinkle with parsley.

For linguine with poached chicken in Marsala, place 2 boneless, skinless chicken breasts in a pan and pour over 100 ml (3½ fl oz) Marsala and enough chicken stock to cover, then poach gently for 15 minutes or until just cooked through. Meanwhile, cook and drain the linguine and fry the mushrooms as above. Cut the chicken into strips and stir through the drained pasta with the mushrooms, a little of the poaching liquid (boiled down if liked) to loosen and some double cream. Serve at once. **Total cooking time 20 minutes.**

index

acknowledgements

Commissioning editor: Eleanor Maxfield
Designer: Tracy Killick
Editor: Alex Stetter
Assistant production manager: Caroline Alberti

Photography: Octopus Publishing Group Stephen Conroy
52-53, 108-109, 165, 181, 195, 201; Will Heap 1, 4-5, 7,
8, 29, 113, 115, 117, 119, 121, 125, 127, 129, 131, 133,
137, 139, 141, 143, 149, 151, 153, 175, 193, 211, 219,
221, 229, 231; Lis Parsons 2-3, 6, 9, 10-11, 13, 15, 17, 19,
21, 23, 25, 31, 33, 39, 41, 43, 45, 47, 49, 51, 55, 57, 59, 61,
63, 65, 69, 71, 73, 75, 77, 79, 81, 83, 85, 87, 89, 91, 93, 95,
97, 99, 101, 103, 105, 107, 123, 135, 145, 147, 154-155,
159, 163, 171, 179, 183, 187, 191, 204-205, 207, 217, 227;
William Reavell 35, 37, 111, 161, 177, 209; Craig Robertson
213, 223, 233; William Shaw 27, 67, 157, 167, 169, 173,
185, 189, 197, 199, 203, 215, 225.